3 STEPS TO HIMALAYAS

A Practical Guide to Achieve Your Goals

Ramesh Kundu

Invincible Publishers

First published in India in 2018

ISBN: 978-93-88333-32-0

Invincible Publishers

G-120, Sushant Lok III, Sector 57, Gurgaon-122002

Registered Address: Opposite Kasturba Ashram,
Radaur, Haryana–135133

Printed at Thomson Press (India) LTD

Dedicated to Shakti aka Sudhir Thakran - a rebel who never shied away from any challenge, be it physical or mental, despite being dealt a short hand in the form of polio and being snatched away from us at a young age of 19. The world is not the same without him.

Acknowledgement

Niharika – a talented daughter, who never hesitates to hold a mirror in front of me.

Pradeep Kataria – a gem of a person, who always makes you forget what stress is.

Ashwini Choudhary – a master storyteller,who makes you look at the larger picture.

Sandeep Sindhu – a wise young man, who finds a simple solution for every complex problem.

Iesh Pratap Singh – a business monk, who always makes you look at the brighter side of life.

A special thanks to **Neelam,** my wife, who supported me with her hard saved money to get this book published.

Thanks to **Ajay Setia** of Invincible Publishers for making this book a reality.

DISCLAIMER

This book narrates true incidents, historical facts and stories as the author remembers them best. Some names have been changed to protect personal identities. The author does not claim absolute accuracy of the events shared here.

CONTENTS

Introduction

This book is an attempt to look at simple solutions for multiple challenges we come across in life. Students, job seekers, employed professionals, entrepreneurs, etc. face one common hurdle in achieving their goals – limiting beliefs. Our self-awareness (inside out) and social awareness (outside in) can help us overcome our limiting beliefs, and in turn the challenges faced by us.

What makes us humans different from other species is our power of imagination, ability to work together in large groups, and competing with others for more and more of everything. Right from childhood, we are taught to compete for doing better in studies, sports and even our professions. We are always either at war with others or ourselves to attain a leadership position in our own world. Different people have different weapons to fight this constant ongoing war, and success not only depends on fighting it better every time, but also on deciding when to step back, when to ignore the gauntlet thrown at us, and when to be just silent and wait for the right moment.

The quality of our life depends upon the decisions we make in fighting this war. Decisions taken by us in past have made it possible for us to be where we are today, and today's decisions will decide our tomorrow. As every one of us wants to do better in life, the road which leads us to our goals is improving our decision-making, which includes having control over our emotions and taking on situations as they evolve. Our decisions are bound to go wrong if we are rigid in our approach and form prejudices about people and situations.

Let us start our journey to the Himalayas with an open mind.

3 Steps To Himalayas

The First Step Is To Know Yourself

We look at the world in our own extension to make sense of it; so it is imperative to know the self-first. We think we know ourselves, but would be surprised to find how little we actually do. And I am not talking about our gender, age, qualification, profession, designation, assets etc but who we are individually.

In fact, even whatever we know about others is very little and of no consequence. We just know the historical facts, dates, decisions made etc., but are we aware of the thoughts and strategies that went behind those decisions? Only such information can help us in not only knowing others but also learning from it and improving our own decision making as well.

If an individual is asked to speak about others, one may speak about few minutes, but when asked about the self, one does not have much to say. That is how much we know ourselves. If we know about ourselves – our beliefs and value systems, likes and dislikes, passions and preferences, strengths and areas of improvement, our competencies and skills; it will become way easier to deal with our environment and brings clarity of our goals in life.

The Second Is To Know About Himalayas (Your Goals)

The second most important thing is to know that which lies outside of us; how things are changing – socially, technologically, economically and legally. Being aware of what is happening around us in this constantly changing world helps us base our decisions knowledge based, and not on the suggestions of others with vested interests. Most of the times we form goals based on suggestions of others and not on what we want from our lives.

Knowing ourselves brings clarity on what we believe in, what is our purpose in life and what we are good at. Knowing our environment helps us in finding the place where we would be successful and happy. It is basically finding a match between what we love and demand for our skill sets or creating a demand if it doesn't exist already.

While basing our decisions for goals we want to pursue, we need to look at relevant and verified information, facts, and our knowledge; as in this age of 'Google' there is lot of easily available misleading, irrelevant and unverified information. Mis information can cost us a lot, be it the time of war or peace.

The Third Is To Find Out How Passionate You Are To Get There

Passion is our life's driving force. Knowing our passion in life gives us something to build the rest of our life around. It is something that challenges and motivates us; it is what we think about when we go to sleep and motivates us when we wake up. It's something for which we are willing to sacrifice leisure and pleasures for.

Finding it:

Being aware of what we enjoy most about our lives can help us define our passion.

Ask these 3 simple questions to find your passion:

1. What would I like to do even if I am not paid for it?
2. Doing what excites me?
3. What it is that would never tire me of doing?

Developing it:

Competence, creativity and making an impact can help in pursuing our passion. It requires time to develop the skills and competencies to pursue it. For example, it may take years to improve our writing skills and establish ourselves in the publishing industry before the income, opportunities and success come our way.

Enjoying it:

Passion is the thread which connects all things we enjoy doing in our lives. And the satisfaction we get from doing what we are passionate about is bliss. Since we enjoy doing things we are passionate about, we feel more committed to keep on doing it as it brings up our energy level.

Chalking Out A Strategy And Then Working On It To Get There Is The Easier Part

Most times, we fail to follow through with our decisions because of their complexity; keeping the solutions simple helps. If we can describe life in three points: Brahma, Vishnu and Mahesh, i.e., the creator, the protector and the destroyer; time – past, present and future; matter – gas, liquid and solid, then why can't we find a solution to our day-to-day challenges in three steps too?

In this book, real experiences of life have been put down and analyzed in a simple form or told through historical facts or stories; followed by learning from those and a three-step solution.

Chapter 1

Dealing With Stress

"We are a result of our decisions; yesterday's decisions made us what we are today, and today's decisions will decide our tomorrow."

The one aspect common to all species that are alive is an instinct for SURVIVAL–an inbuilt mechanism of the fear to survive. The fear of physical harm helps us save ourselves from dangerous situations, but the psychological fear is our own imagination in the form of the fear of failure, fear of what people might think or say about us, fear of failing the expectations of our parents, teachers, bosses, spouse, etc.

The second most common trait in us, and a negative one at that, is anger. We react in anger and then live in the fear of reprisal from others. We often take decisions in anger which come back to haunt us, or we often say things in anger which begets a feeling of guilt in us.

The third most common negative trait is greed. Under the influence of greed, we take decisions which make us poorer financially or wreck our relations. Over time, it makes us stand alone, devoid of a social support system which is necessary for our mental and physical wellbeing.

All of this is encompassed in limiting beliefs. Decisions gone wrong in the past make us hesitant to take decisions today. Times change, our skills and competencies change, our knowledge and attitude change. What didn't work in the past may very well work in the present. Let us not limit our beliefs by the chains of unsuccessful attempts made earlier.

These are the reasons behind our stress. We remain stressed at our workplace because of the fear of our bosses, fear of unreasonable expectations, fear of failure, fear of losing our job, fear of the unpredictable future. We also stress over reasons and elements beyond our control. We often get stressed out due to unreasonable expectations of our family members, and at times of the community/society.

To safeguard our emotional state, we create a cocoon of fear around us, even though most of it is simply imaginative. Over time, we get used to this comfortable zone. Fear paralyzes us and stops us from taking any action – we feel safer this way.

If we want to live a stress-free life, we have to understand ourselves (self-awareness), manage ourselves in relation to the world at large (self-management), and develop ourselves for the little known tomorrow (self-development).

We have to look at our passions and skillsets, and find/create opportunities for what we are good at. Some people are good fighters, some are good strategists, some make innovative weapons, while others profit from war. A war is not just weapons and bodies; what's equally important in a war is proper clothing, transportation, rations, propaganda and support from the local population.

To live a stress-free life, we have to understand and face our fears, explore the reasons behind our limiting beliefs, have control on our anger and suppress our greed.

And it is just as simple as it sounds. Life can only be simple if we keep it that way. If we let our lives be controlled by external factors, it will become complex, uncertain and full of stress. Let us take charge of it and make it worth living.

One thing that has worked with me in this regard is adding as many positive habits to my life as possible, so that there is no time or space for negative thoughts or habits. It is very difficult to change our unhealthy habits. In fact, we always desire change but are unable to work on it — just like our New Year resolutions for taking better care of our health come and go every year.

The second most important thing is keep our expectations real. Here, I am talking about the expectations we build in relation to other people or the outcome of situations. We cannot expect tigers to turn vegetarian or turn things in our favour just because our intentions are good.

Thirdly, we should take care of the company we keep. Seek out positive and mature people to have around you and you shall find a lot of strength in them. Positive people bring along a lot of positive energy, which translates to forming positive habits. Our outlook slowly changes towards ourselves and the world around us, conditioned by the company we keep. Build relationships where you don't have to think twice before expressing your views or feel hesitant in getting feedback for your words and actions.

This gives us a clear direction and speed towards our goals in life – to reach the Himalayas.

Chapter 2

The Success Table

Success table:

Self	Family	Society
Self-Development	Faith	Passion
Self-Management	Family	Perseverance
Self-Awareness	Fun	Priority

Please tick-mark one of the three choices given in each of the nine parameters below. Please be truthful and mark the closest choice that you think applies to you.

Self-Awareness:

a. I know my likes/dislikes, preferences, strengths and areas of improvement

b. I know what motivates me

c. I know what kind of life I want to live

Self-Management:

a. I am aware of my emotions, but am unable to control them at times

b. I am able to control my emotions as the situation demands

c. I always respond with a peaceful and calm mind

Self-Development:

a. I am aware of my areas that require development and work on it in a planned way

b. I can visualize the competency requirement for the near future and seek opportunities to develop them

c. I work on my limiting beliefs in a planned way

Fun:

a. I see fun in most of my daily activities

b. I seek fun even in challenging activities

c. I approach every challenge with a fun quotient

Family:

a. I like to be around my family/friends

b. I draw my strength from my family/friends

c. I always stand up for my family/friends

Faith:

a. Faith in self

b. Faith in family/friends

c. Faith in society

Priority:

a. My priorities are clear regarding managing time

b. My priorities are clear on myself/family/work

c. My priorities are clear on the to find time for society

Perseverance:

a. I work diligently till I come across a hurdle

b. I work till I come to a conclusive end

c. I work for my target with full faith, even if everybody else thinks it is not prudent

Passion:

a. My passion about people and things keeps changing
b. I work with full passion when I have set my mind about something
c. I forget about everything else when I work on something I am passionate about

Take your score as 1 for every 'a', 2 for every 'b', and 3 for every 'c'. Add up your score and divide the total by 9.

The Five Stages:

First Stage - On the path to success: If your score is upto 1.33.

Second Stage - Moderately successful: If your score is more than 1.33 upto 2.

Third Stage - Successful: If your score is more than 2 upto 2.66.

Fourth Stage - Highly successful: If your score is more than 2.66, but less than 3.

Fifth Stage - Exceptionally successful: If your score is 3.

Higher the score, the more likely you are to be successful in your field.

Chapter 3

Beliefs And Value Systems

"It is never right versus wrong; it is always my right versus your right."

3.1 Our beliefs and value systems:

There are two parallel train tracks passing by the outskirts of a town. One is in use while the other was discarded many years back. It is evening time and some kids are playing on these tracks. Since it is not uncommon for trains in India to run late, these kids have no idea at what time a train may come. On track "A" which is in use, some ten kids are playing, while on track "B" which has not been in use, a lone child is present.

The question is, if you are the person in charge of changing tracks for the train on that line, provided that track B is usable, where would you direct the train to, knowing very well that it can't be stopped? If you let the train continue on track "A" it is certain that the ten kids would die, and if you direct it to track "B", the only kid playing on it would die.

Like many other ethical dilemmas, there is no right or wrong answer here.

More than 80% of people to whom I asked this question said that they would direct the train to track "B" and sacrifice the one kid to save ten kids. Now, if we look at it from the right and wrong perspective, should we sacrifice the one intelligent kid who chose to play on the unused track over the other ten who should have known the risk involved very well.

What we decide is based on our beliefs and value systems.

Also, this is how our democracy works.

The three important systems we need to understand are:

a. Our Beliefs

b. Our Values

c. Our Goals

1. What are my limiting beliefs?

a. What stops me from achieving what I want to?

b. How self-aware am I?

c. What is my self-image?

2. What are my value systems?

a. Which actions make me happy?

b. What has made me proud?

c. When do I feel uncomfortable?

3. What are my goals in life?

a. What is my purpose of living this life?

b. Do my goals match my beliefs and value systems?

c. Do my goals excite me?

"Our worst enemy is limitation of our own mind."

3.2 Achieving in unfavorable conditions:

In 401 BC, Cyrus, the brother of a Persian king, recruited thousands of Greeks fighters as mercenaries in the Persian army to quell rebellion in parts of Persia. However, he had a parallel plan and purpose to unseat his brother and becoming the king himself.

The two armies met near Babylon and Cyrus was killed early in the battle, and his army lost the war. The situation suddenly became precarious for the Greeks. They were at the mercy of the hostile Persians now; but to their relief, the king Ataxerxes conveyed that neither would he order to kill them nor imprison them, as that would have been the punishment of having fought against him. Instead, he wanted them to leave Persia at the earliest, and appointed one of his trusted commanders as envoy to escort them through Persia.

The king also had an alternate plan to lead Greeks deep into hostile territory and leave them at the mercy of Persian enemies and harsh nature. They had to travel more than 2,400 kilometres to reach their homes.

A difficult route and insufficient supplies made it clear to the Greeks how difficult their journey was going to be. When a Greek commander expressed his concern, he was called to a meeting along with his officers to sort it out, and all were ordered to be beheaded. One officer escaped somehow and informed his countrymen of this treachery. They got together for a meeting, but only chaos, arguments, accusations and despair were the outcome. That night, one amongst them–Xenophon, a philosopher and a man of standing, saw death in his dream.

The next day, he called upon all the remaining officers for a meeting and laid bare the situation. He evoked their Gods, their superior fighting abilities, and their families waiting for them back home. He aroused their anger towards their common enemy – the Persians, and asked them to focus on their dream – to reach Greece and be with their families. "Greeks, mountains and rivers are not our enemies, our own muddled state of mind is. If we let go of our ego, lighten our belongings, move fast and fight the Persians as one, we will reach home sooner. Let there be no more arguments, let us learn from our mistakes, adapt to the terrain, live off the land and have an absolute clarity and purpose regarding our goal."

Bound with one aim, they resumed their journey, avoided the Persian army troops, moved at night and rested through the day to finally make it to their motherland.

The biggest enemy is our own mind...

How do humans achieve?

a. Power of imagination

b. Quality of being able to work together in large numbers

c. Competitive spirit

The power of imagination (myths) unites us as nations, organisations, religions, communities, and families. This enables us to work together in very large numbers resulting in scientific discoveries, technology, medical advancements, artificial intelligence, and so on.

A lion doesn't compete with other lions for the maximum number of kills; it only kills for hunger; humans, on the other hand, compete with each other to be better in all fields. This makes us always hungry for more. Being competitive lets us create new opportunities.

But this hunger for more also brings stress...

"Always remember, stressing out physically or mentally doesn't kill you; stressing out in both at the same time will."

3.3 Health and stress:

Ranjan Das, CEO and MD of SAP-Indian Subcontinent, died after a massive cardiac arrest in Mumbai in 2017; he was only 42.

Ranjan was a workaholic, an active sportsman, a fitness freak and a marathon runner. One fine morning, after his workout, he collapsed due to a massive heart attack and died.

The question arises as to why an exceptionally active athletic person succumbed to a heart attack at merely 42 years of age.

The answer lies in his lifestyle; due to his challenging work, he used to manage his day with only 4-5 hours of sleep. Individuals who sleep less than 5 hours a night have a three-fold increased risk of suffering a heart attack. Even one night of sleep loss increases the level of toxic substances in our body such as Interleukin-6, TNF-alpha and C-reactive protein which increase the chances of cancer, arthritis and heart disease.

Barring stress control, Ranjan Das did everything right. He ate proper food, exercised, and maintained proper weight, but he missed getting proper and adequate sleep, which is a minimum of seven hours.

Today more people die from stress than hunger...

What is killing humans?

We are becoming more and more like machines…

a. Distancing ourselves from nature – causing pollution
b. Our lifestyle, i.e., eating habits and physical activities
c. Engaging in the virtual world – contributing to our stress level

In this super competitive world, we race against time. Our expectations from ourselves are very high, and ultimately we burn ourselves out one day. This stressful lifestyle is killing our emotions and destroying our social support system, as we neither have the time nor the relationships which can abate our stress.

We need to start looking out and balancing out, the sooner the better.

"Merely breaking a rule is no achievement; breaking it and coming out unhurt is one."

3.4 Rules are meant to be broken:

This incident happened in a small city in Haryana.

A *seth* was running late to catch a train to Delhi. His neighbour was a Choudhary who had a bike. Seth knew that his only chance to catch the train was to find a fast driver with a two wheeler. Traffic is chaotic at its best in small cities and towns. After telling his problem to his neighbour, he requested him to take him to the railway station. Seeing this as a challenge, the Choudhary agreed.

He kicked his bike alive and took off like a bullet. Seth almost fell off, but managed to remain seated by grabbing Choudhary by his waist. His speedy and reckless driving worried the Seth to his core and he cursed himself for having took such a risk. He couldn't get off at this point either for the fear of suffering ridicule by his neighbour for the rest of his life.

Thus, he kept telling Choudhary to go slower, as he was certain that he would catch his train. But when Choudhary accelerated even more, Seth felt completely helpless. As the traffic signal just ahead turned red, Seth let out a momentary sigh of relief. Seeing the red signal, Choudhary accelerated even more. When Seth asked him to pull the brakes for the red signal, Choudhary assured him not to worry and asked him to sit tight. He crossed the red signal faster than a bullet, and…nothing happened. They continued this way for another half a kilometre. Again came a traffic signal with a red light, again

Seth told Choudhary to stop his bike, and again he told him not to worry and sit tight. Seth felt worried now that he might never even return home alive, let alone reaching the railway station. He closed his eyes and started invoking his Gods as the bike crossed another red signal at breakneck speed.

After another kilometre, they came across another traffic signal, but it was green this time. Seth was happy as they were very close to the railway station now. He felt sure to catch his train. Happily, he told Choudhary to speed up before the signal turned red. Choudhary braked hard at the signal and stopped the bike. Seth was confused, and asked, "Choudhary *sahib*, now what? The signal is green, we can cross without a problem."

Choudhary looked back at Seth and smiled, "Seth ji, do you take me for a fool? How can I cross now? What if somebody like me is coming at full speed from the other side? You want us dead or what?"

This story defines one's risk taking capacity and how the world works. Problems exist in the way we look at them.

Taking risks:

a. Without taking any risk, it is difficult to achieve our goals

b. Taking unnecessary risks can bring harm

c. Taking calculated risks in line with our goals takes us closer to success

Risk taking capacity varies from person to person; some take risks for no reason at all and some are risk averse. While taking a risk, we should think about three things; first – is it necessary? Second – what are the best and worst case scenarios? And third – whether is it in line with our goals. Here, the best case scenario was that Seth would catch his train, but the worst case scenario was a serious accident. Taking calculated risks to achieve our life's goals is prudent.

Take only calculated risks which are in line with achieving your goals...

"We always end up finding reasons to support our beliefs."

3.5:- A Russian and two vodkas:

In mid-eighties, a manager of a bar in Moscow was confused by a customer who would come every evening, sit alone and order two Vodkas, then take a sip from each simultaneously. He observed this for more than a week before he thought of approaching him to solve this mystery.

"Well, I have a very close friend with whom I always used to drink, but since he is posted out in Siberia, we cannot do it together anymore. I feel like I am drinking with him whenever I drink from both the glasses simultaneously," the customer replied. The manager nodded in appreciation and thanked him for sharing that personal information.

This continued on for a few more months. The customer would come, take a particular table in the corner and order drinks in batches of two.

Then one day, the manager observed that the customer had ordered and was drinking from only one glass. He approached him with growing concern on his face, took a seat opposite him and said, "I am so sorry for your loss."

"Sorry for what?" the customer asked.

"That your friend is no more," the manager replied.

"Who told you that? I spoke to him just an hour back, and he is hale and hearty," the customer said.

"Oh, since you were drinking from only one glass today, I assumed the worst," the manager said apologetically.

"Oh, this? This is because my liver does not support my drinking habit anymore, and the doctor has strictly said NO to me drinking. You see, it is only my friend drinking today, not me."

"We only looks for reasons to strengthen our beliefs for decisions already taken".

Important things we live by:

a. Feelings

b. Faith

c. Facts

Our decisions are flawed most times as we don't look at things as they are, but as we want to see them. If a boss likes someone in his/her team and that person makes a mistake, the pet reply is, 'How would somebody learn if they don't try.' The same mistake if made by someone he/she doesn't like, the boss would say, 'It was such a small matter, he/she is good for nothing.' When our feelings and facts say different things, we should go with facts and not feelings. Decisions based on facts are constant, whereas decisions based on feelings can cause extreme consequences.

When our feelings dictate our decisions, chances are that they are flawed...

"The time taken to reach you goal depends on your direction and speed."

3.6 The Wise Man:

Once upon a time in the fourteenth century, a wise man was standing at the crossroads in a market when a traveller approached him and asked, "I am travelling to so and so village and it is getting dark. Can you tell me how much time it would take me to reach there?" The wise man shook his head and the traveller carried on.

After the traveller had walked about 50 yards away, the wise man called him back and told him that it would take him around one hour to reach there. The traveller was not amused. He said, "Are you a fool to call me back after I had covered more than 50 yards, to tell me something you could have told me when I asked you in the first place?"

The wise man told him he wanted to be certain about the information the traveller wanted. "I know the distance between this place and your destination, but the time taken to cover that distance would depend upon two things; direction and speed. Since I have seen now that you took the right direction as well as how fast you walk, I can say for certain that you will take one hour to reach there. Some people take much less time, while some much more. Also your speed depends on your urgency and as it is getting dark now, so you would walk faster than normal. All these things indicate that you would safely reach your destination within the time I just shared with you. Carry on now, I wish you a safe journey."

"Our outcomes depend upon the situation, the direction taken and our speed".

What we need to reach a goal:

a. Direction

b. Speed

c. Resources

Our speed depends upon our urgency to finish a task, our direction on our knowledge, and the resources on our passion to get there. If we are passionate about something, resources can be arranged. We need all these to achieve our goals. There are times we can afford to relax regarding one or more aspects, and at other times we cannot take any chances.

If our direction and speed are right, we can achieve our goals within the decided timelines...

"Choose your career based on your passion; else try to find passion in what you do"

3.7 What career to choose?

One of my friends joined as an IPS in the early nineties, an ideal job at that time. One could do a lot for the society or the self, depending on one's personal beliefs/value systems. He was doing pretty well, co-authored a book with a well-known personality on digital governance, and was even invited by a well-known French management college for his management degree on full scholarship.

Within a few years, however, he decided to leave the services as he was not comfortable with the way things worked in the police department. Coming from a small town, this kind of a job was a dream, but what went wrong?

Well, he has a very creative mind, and the first casualty in disciplined forces like the army or police is creativity. The first thing one is taught here is discipline – taking orders from superiors without any questions. It was as simple as that. His passion didn't lie there, and if you are not passionate about your profession, you are bound to feel frustrated at some point of time. The only exception could be when you change your core values and accept defeat.

I asked him, "What happened? It was a damn good job with power, status and good financial rewards."

"Nothing, it's indeed a good job, but it was not aligned with my goals in life. I will be better off where my beliefs and value systems match my profession," was all he said in response.

He started with an NGO and is a subject matter expert now. He works as an advisor to many governmental organisations and delivers lectures all over the world.

He is happy for his decision…

What career to choose?

a. What am I passionate about?

b. What am I good at?

c. Is there a demand or can I create a demand of what I am good at/passionate about?

Career is not just earning enough money to live, it is an alignment of what you value, what you are passionate about, what you are good at, and matching with the demands or creating demands for your skillset. If you do something you love, your work will never be a burden. It will always be a joy that will not only bring happiness but also fulfilment in your life.

Find an occupation that matches your passion, and you shall be happy for life.

"It is the fear of death which kills you, not death itself–it liberates you."

3.8 The leopard incident – just another day in Tea:

One of my friends, Devender Chauhan, was managing a tea estate near Jorhat in Assam. Since there are quite a few wildlife sanctuaries in upper Assam, wild elephants and leopards are very common to visit the surrounding areas. Normally, elephants are lured by jackfruits and rice toddy, whereas leopards by dogs and goats; but there were always exceptions.

Devender was in his office when he was informed that a leopard had attacked a couple of his workers. He asked his driver to get his vehicle immediately to visit the accident site and get medical care to the injured at the earliest. When he reached the spot, he found around 150 workers gathered already and were helping the victims. A crowd also discourages leopards who are thieves by nature. Some paramedics had also reached there by this time and were helping the injured to an ambulance.

Devender was giving instructions to the people present there when he suddenly became aware of a peculiar smell in the air. Fearing that the leopard might be back, he turned around quickly, but the animal was already in the air by then. A claw went slicing through his shoulder and he staggered back. Within a few seconds, both were on the ground. Everybody else scattered away with shouts and warnings. When people turned around, they saw that Devender was lying on his back, and the leopard was on top of him. Devender's hands were around the leopard's neck. He shouted at his armed guards (due to insurgency, many companies had deployed armed guards trained by the Assam police) to take aim and kill the leopard before it killed him. The guards were hesitant for two reasons; first, for their own safety, and second, it was a very risky shot and could kill their boss instead. Devender and the leopard were still struggling when a guard drew closer to them to get a good aim, then shot the leopard in the head and killed him.

More people came forward for the rescue and took the wounded Devender to a hospital. He was soon flown out to Kolkata.

He had torn legs and shoulders, and was operated on multiple times. He remained at the hospital for around seven months, and took about two years to completely recover and return back to his normal routine.

Later he told us that ravenous look in the eyes of the leopard made him realize that either it was leopard or him; there was only one way and that was to fight for his life.

It is our instinct to survive which makes us fierce in our fight for life. If we let fear take control of our emotions in such situations, we may never see the light of next day. And our beliefs of our strength and control on negative emotions can only help us in such impossible situations.

How to be emotionally strong?

a. Self-awareness: Understand your beliefs, values, preferences and strengths

b. Social awareness: Understand others' emotions and reactions

c. Self-Motivation: Understand the need to be strong and positive in the face of adversity

In a given situation of emergency, different people react in different ways. It is a matter of our reflexes which depend on our mind preparation. Everybody fears for survival, but when it comes to fighting for life, only a few fight like hell. Our strength built over a number of years and ingrained in our minds comes to the rescue, and we strive to survive to achieve our goals and spend more time with our loved ones. Even death staring right at us becomes a small problem in comparison then. When you can't make a line smaller, just draw a bigger line next to it.

Our beliefs & value systems decide our degree of motivation.

Chapter 4

Emotions

"When our decisions are clouded by emotions, our future gets clouded by uncertainty."

4.1 Largest manmade famine:

An estimated thirty-six million Chinese starved to death in the years between 1958 and 1961, while forty million others failed to be born. It was a manmade disaster and a glaring example of failed leadership. This famine occurred neither during a war nor a period of natural calamity. It was rather the result of one man's ego.

A decade after the Communist party came to power in China, Mao Zedong vowed to build a communist paradise through sheer revolutionary zeal, collectivising farmland and creating massive communes at an astonishing speed. In 1958, he launched 'The Great Leap Forward', a plan to modernise the entire Chinese economy which was so ambitious that it tipped over into insanity. Not satisfied with being the most powerful man in China, he wanted to be the leader of the international communist movement. If the Soviet Union believed it could catch up to the US in fifteen years, he vowed, China could overtake Britain in production in no time. His vicious attacks on other leaders who dared to voice concern cowed down opposition.

Mao's policies drove the peasants from their individual small holdings. Working communally, they were now forced to yield almost everything to the state, either to feed the cities or to increase exports to make sure that the outside world saw China in a different light. The peasants were allotted enough grain just for their survival for a short period.

Mao pronounced that family, in the new order of collective farming, was no longer necessary. This sudden change in the system without enough time and planning led the grain production to plummet and the communal kitchen system to collapse.

The plan proved a disaster from the beginning. Local officials, either from fanaticism or fear, sent grossly exaggerated reports of their success to the centre, proclaiming harvests three or four times the actual production. Huge amounts of grain had to be despatched to cities and exported as well. Party cadres harassed or killed those who sought to tell the truth and covered up these deaths.

In Henan province, one in eight people were wiped out by starvation and brutality during that period of three years, forty-four of a village's forty-five inhabitants died; the last remaining resident, a woman in her 60s, went insane. Others were tortured, beaten or buried alive for declaring realistic harvests, refusing to hand over what little food they had, stealing scraps or simply enraging the officials. When people died in a family, they didn't bury the person because they could still collect their food rations. They kept the bodies in bed and covered them up while the corpses were eaten by mice; people ate corpses and fought for the bodies.

Ruthlessness ran through the system. Those who tried to escape the famine were rounded up; many died of starvation or from brutality at the detention centres. Police hunted down those who wrote anonymous letters raising alarm.

"To distribute resources evenly will only ruin the Great Leap Forward," Mao warned his colleagues. "When there is not enough to eat, people starve to death. It is better to let half the people die so that others can eat their fill."

Emotions we should control:

These are some inherent emotions that we should learn how to control.

a. Hate

b. Greed

c. Fear

When we have absolute power, we feel we can afford to sacrifice people for our grand schemes. Greed makes us want to have more of everything – name and fame. Our hate towards the opposition silences the voice of reason and our fear to lag behind makes us ruthless. We start keeping around us people who don't have opinions of their own, but carry out our commands at any cost. This is the price we pay and the result is catastrophic.

The first casualty of power is the voice of reason.

"Your winning or losing a battle doesn't depend on just your fear, but on your enemy's as well."

"Fear brings attack and domination; evoking fear in others can bring a win without a fight"

4.2 The fear of numbers:

It must be around four in the afternoon when I came across Maan at the DAV college hostel in Chandigarh. It was my first year in college and Maan was a new friend. He was agitated and angry that afternoon.

I knew that he liked a girl from the adjoining Home Science college. I asked him, "Hi Maan, what happened? Why are you so serious? Has that girl slapped you?"

He kept quiet for a few moments, then said, "No, not her, but her boyfriend." The girl's boyfriend had indeed slapped Maan when he was trying to speak to her. Maan was angry and wanted revenge. "Kundu yaar, had he slapped me when I was alone might still have been bearable, but in front of the girl, and for what? I didn't misbehave at all. Brother, you have to help me teach that bastard a lesson."

"Forget it yaar, the girl you like has a boyfriend. Forget about her and her boyfriend as well. There are so many beautiful girls around, Chandigarh is full of pretty damsels. I am sure you will find someone else, and better than that one. Carry on buddy, the world doesn't stop here. Besides, what will you achieve by slapping him back? Do you even know who he is, where he lives, what his name is?" Maan didn't seem convinced by my words, but carried on.

The next evening, it was almost dark when he came to my room all excited. "Yaar, I have found out where he stays, it's close by."

"What are you talking about?"

"The person who slapped me yesterday, yaar. How can you forget so soon?" Maan sensed my apprehension of us getting outnumbered by his friends and him, and said, "I have done the *reckki* too, he is alone as of now. Let us not waste time, get up yaar. He comes from Patiala to see her. If we miss him now, may never come across him again."

I knew he would drag me in any case, so I got ready to face the unknown challenge. My roommate also volunteered to come. 'No way,' I thought. He was good for nothing and would have been a liability. He couldn't even run fifty yards, if the situation demanded. "No, no way, you stay here, we are not going to watch a movie," I told him, but his excitement had turned him deaf to my warnings. To Maan, it seemed nothing less than a bonus. "Good," he said. "Let's go."

Maan led us to the north east side of college. There was a small plot of open space, beyond which a row of houses started. Maan called out the boy's name in front of a house. When nothing happened, I did the same but more loudly. Someone came out and yelled, "What is it? Who the hell is shouting?" When he emerged from the house, the first thing noticeable was his height & built- least 6'4" tall with body of a wrestler.

'Maan is a bastard for putting us in this pickle. He should have told us what we were up against. We are fucked royally today,' I thought. In no way could we think of beating him, but hoped to simply return in one piece. This bulky man who seemed double our weight could easily have picked up two of us by the collar and hurled us at the third; game over. There was no doubt in my mind that I wouldn't spare Maan after this.

"What do you want?" he again asked.

None of us spoke for a few seconds. At last, Maan gathered the courage and said, "You slapped me the other day!' He spared no expletives either, as anger had completely consumed him and his reason. I felt a little hesitation on the wrester's side. 'This is the time to save our asses,' I thought.

"Listen up, pahalwan. If the three of us beat you to pulp, you would complain that you were outnumbered. Do one thing, come to the General Hostel of GCM and ask anyone about me – Choudhary. And if you don't have the balls to come to my place, tell a place and time of your choosing and I'll be there," I continued.

Darkness was already setting in, making it difficult to read expressions, which was of great help as we wouldn't otherwise have been able to get away with fear written so clearly on our faces.

His shoulders slackened a bit. "What do you want, Choudhary bhai?" he asked.

"Nothing much. You slapped him for no reason the other day, now he will slap you–simple," I said.

The guy shook his head.

"Seriously, do you want to get beaten up badly? It's your choice now, one slap or two broken legs. Say sorry and put your hands behind you to take a slap.

"Okay, I am sorry," he said and put his hands behind him as ordered. I nodded to Maan and he gave him a tight slap. After that, we walked away, just like that.

This is how it works at times, you have to win over your opponents on a psychological level. I took a name which was not mine, mentioned a hostel where I was not staying, knowing that this name and hostel both had a reputation–one that saved us.

Overcome your fear:

a. Fear of physical harm: It is built in our system and is necessary for survival. Accept it.

b. Psychological fear: It is in our imagination, the fear of being a failure, being wrong, being ridiculed – look at 'limiting beliefs'.

c. Work on your fears

Winning a race depends not only on you, but your competitors as well. If you seem fearless, your opponents may back down–making you the victor by default. Never lower down your guard, as history is full of examples when weaker sides in terms of military won battles and wars. Surprise, faster movement, unleashing a new weapon, or perception of strength may turn sides.

To win in an unfavorable situation, strike at your opponent's biggest weakness with your strongest weapon...

"Fear is a natural emotion; accepting it is the first step to overcome it."

4.3 Lockout notice:

My first job in Tea was in Tripura in the early nineties. A porous border with Bangladesh, huge paddy fields and only 3′ high pillars separating the two countries allowed criminals to cross over easily to other side, so the crime rate and corruption were also high in this area. It was a politically sensitive area and had a laid back work culture, due to the influence of left.

The tea estate management had bought this property a couple of years back and wanted to turn it around. After putting tough people at the right places, they decided to go for a lockout–a tactic to wake people up from their slumber.

The first challenge was to put up notices of the lockout at the office and the factory. Most tea estates are in the hinterland with bad roads. Small towns around with a small police force are of not much help, in addition to the insurgency making their movement even more difficult. It was not possible to simply put up a notice at office, declaring lockout, wherein a thousand or more people would be out of work with no alternate employment available and their families would be without food. Tea has always had a violent workforce, which has resulted in fatalities at times, so it was decided to put up the notice at night.

Parminder and I were given this risky task at around 8 PM for the same night, and we sat down with a drink each to formulate a strategy. "There is only one road, but we can't take the risk of using it both ways. It is too risky as there is an out division on the way and if they come to know of it somehow, we are done for," Parminder said.

I knew if they were to catch us, we might not see our families and friends ever again. They could attack us with poisoned arrows, homemade guns or simply chopping knives. "We can take some parallel dirt road, but it goes through the tribal belt," I said. There were two problems here; one, we didn't know if there was a parallel path that connected with the main road ahead, and second, the tribals might not like the intrusion at all. Out of these two, the second option was a little less frightful so we decided to go for it.

A decision was yet to be made regarding the time. I suggested, "Since the factory closes at midnight, the best time to reach there would be around 11:45 PM and hide in the nursery to see if somehow they have got a hint of the Management's decision for a loc-kout." Hardly anything was unknown to the workers — drivers, cooks and a horde of other servants were always around, and only a word's slip from someone was enough.

"We cannot take our bike there either. We will have to cover the last few hundred yards on foot pushing the bike and then find a place to hide it before we go in," Parminder suggested. Since there were no other motor vehicles in that part of the village, a Yamaha bike could be heard from a long distance away, particularly at night.

We decided to start at around 10:45, taking ample buffer for an unknown road where we could find dead ends or get stuck. The area was very sparsely populated, and the sun sets around five during winters, so no luck in asking our way around.

The third problem was to keep the lockout notices dry, as it started drizzling. Fortunately, we had raincoats. We kept two small swords on either side of the bike, between the shockers and the rear wheel, just in case we had to fight it out with the locals or workers for our lives. We were all set for an adventure.

We downed a couple of drinks before starting out. After navigating through a few dead ends and progressively narrowing paths ending at houses gates, we somehow found a dirt road which led us to the main road to the tea estate. We killed the engine of bike a couple of hundred yards before hiding it in the tea bushes. We had to walk last around 400 yards and we would reach nursery. We listened for a minute or so in the silent night to hear any activity which may indicate that we had been given away. When all seemed clear, we took out our swords and started walking towards the office.

In that area, there were a lot of small rivulets with wooden bridges which allowed only one way movement to cross over. We had overlooked this fact.

Due to our heightened sensory reception brought about with fear, even small sounds got magnified and were scaring us. The partial moonlight enabled us to navigate our way, but it wasn't enough for us to be seen from a distance. We waited for the right moment to cross the bridge, as this was the most vulnerable area for us to get caught. We heaved a sigh of relief as we entered the nursery facing the office, but we knew that it wasn't over till it was over. The actual challenge was to come out from the cover, put up the notices, walk back to our hidden bike and ride back to safety. So many things could go wrong. One person at the wrong time and at wrong place could end it for us with one single shout to his mates.

We looked at each other, wide eyed, a feeble smile on our lips and heart thumping inside our chests. We were both trying hard to hide our fear. Just then, the sound of a siren made us jump. Damn it; It was the shift siren sound, but it had never sounded so loud before. It was time for the workers to return back home; the most frightening few minutes for us.

Workers started coming out, chatting with each other and taking different directions of their labour lines. Our hearts stopped again as a couple of them started walking towards the nursery. 'Oh fuck, have they noticed us?' we thought and looked at one other. Thankfully, they were just looking for a place to pee. Our nerves relaxed a bit.

Within five minutes, the place was entirely quiet again. The factory gates were locked and the figures drifted away in various directions. Only dim sounds of conversation and laughter carried by a soft breeze reached us. The rain had stopped half an hour before. The guards were mobile, making their routine round and checking everything. Then, they sat down in pairs and started smoking. We had to wait for them to go to sleep, and it seemed like it would be a long night for us as well.

Parminder whispered to me, "Doesn't look like we will be able to finish our job today, let us go back." I was certain that we would be sent back if we returned unsuccessful and I didn't want to risk making another trip. "Let us wait for some more time," I finally whispered back.

After about half an hour, the guards strolled away towards the bridge and we got our chance to move. Half bent, we crossed the nursery and reached the office. We put up the notice with glue, only to realise that it had been put upside down. We corrected our mistake with trembling hands, then moved over to the factory gate as quietly as possible to paste a copy on the door. Hearts racing, we turned around to look at the guards who were still at the bridge fortunately.

We returned to the temporary safety of the nursery, as crossing the overbridge was unthinkable. Some loud voices among the guards and a whistle made us shiver. "Have they realized what has happened? Have they recognized us?" I wondered aloud. Since they didn't run towards us, we figured that it was something else, perhaps an argument between them. The whistle was mandatorily blown at regular intervals.

It was 12:35 AM now and our job was done. Not wanting to risk staying back, I told Parminder to follow me towards the back of the nursery. Staying out of the line of vision of the guards, we walked further back and came across the bank of a rivulet. We waded through it, knee deep in water and came across dense thorny bushes lining up on other side. After covering about 50 to 60 yards, we saw a dark opening on one side of it, three meters in height, probably made by goats. It was the kind of tunnel in thorny bushes, but we crawled through it for around 30 feet, come out the other end with a few scratches here and there. From there on, we entered a tea plantation and walked swiftly towards our hidden bike. The uneven land made our walk unsteady, while our eyes hurt from straining too hard to see through the dark and avoid drains that came every 30 feet or so.

Finally, we reached where we had hidden our bike, but it was not there. We looked all around, but to no avail. We even tried to trace back to the place where we had killed the engine and started pushing the bike, but there was still no sign of it. Those were some very frustrating minutes and every little sound made us jump. Finally, we found it parked not far from our track and pushed it for around 300 yards before I jumped on the pillion seat and we drove away. The out division was the only risk now. Parminder wanted to drive as fast as possible, but the terrain was poor, making the bike prone to skidding, so we returned at a reasonable speed of 50 kmph.

The moment we crossed past the danger zone, we yelled our victory in unison, then laughed and sang. After informing our Director who was camping at a nearby tea estate, we decided to have another couple of drinks to sooth our nerves. We could also take the exceptional liberty of not going to office at six the next morning, 'cause we had earned it–damn it.

Fear is natural in all species. We can win over it only by doing things which are fearful in the first place – it's a catch 22 situation, but it is the only way out.

Which habits are important?

a. Passion – energy

b. Discipline

c. Perseverance

There is a lot of noise around us, and we can silence it only by focussing on our job at hand, by working passionately for our goals, by maintaining discipline and perseverance in life till we achieve our goal. The goal may look daunting or dangerous, or others may laugh at it, but if we have the passion, discipline and perseverance for it, we will definitely reach it. Fear is natural, a necessity for our survival, but we can overcome it with these three important values.

If a goal looks big, it means that we are thinking small…

"Relationships are like the trees that provide us shade, wood, flowers and fruits, so need to be nurtured with care and love."

4.4 Investment in relations:

I have always been poor in personal financial investments, but probably earned more by always finding time to spend with my family and friends. Recently, when I made the decision to quit my job and start something of my own, this is what happened:

Three of my friends offered to help me financially, even though I didn't ask for it. Two of my friends offered me a part of their office space in the centre of Gurgaon, including services–all free of cost, and I am using one.

One of my relatives offered me his four bedroom villa at a beautiful location, free of cost, and I am staying in it.

My last landlord did not even mention the 10k that I technically should have paid him as part of the last month's rent — difference between the security I paid him six years ago and the present rent.

My daughter lent support in her own way by limiting her shopping and dine-outs, and reducing her monthly expenditure, although I know how difficult it must be for her.

My parents stayed with me and lent me emotional support.

All this gave me great confidence in myself, my relations, and my new venture. A thank you is not enough for all of them, but they know that I would do the same for them any day.

The lesson learnt is that an investment is necessary, be it financial or even better in relations.

Why to invest in relationships?

a. It provides emotional support

b. It provides financial support in the times of need

c. It helps in self-development by way of knowledge/ experience sharing

We define ourselves as social beings. For thousands of years, we have lived in societies – large groups, and this has helped us in working together for bigger goals. It also gave some of us the freedom to achieve higher order accomplishments in science & technology, and in making social, political and economic reforms. Since our world is very complex and ever changing, things don't always go as per our plan. We need social support during challenging times, and our relationships built over the years are the pillars of strength at such times.

Relationships are like the pillars holding up the structure of your life...

"What others think about you cannot defeat you; what you think of yourself can."

4.5 The price of a chair–accepting criticism:

A farmer named Gopi was once returning from a nearby town with a chair. The bus stop was more than a kilometre from his house, so he picked up the chair, put it on his head and started for his house. He was happy, rather very happy, the chair was a good bargain. "I never thought I could get it for less than a 100 rupees. At eighty, it is a steal."

He had hardly walked fifty steps when he saw Jilley approaching him.

"Shahar gaya tha bhai?" Jilley asked him. (Did you go to town?)

"Haan," Gopi replied. (Yes.)

"Kursi le aaya, kitne ki pari yeh?" (You've got a chair, how much did you pay for it?)

"80 rupees," replied Gopi.

Jilley thought for a few moments, then exclaimed, "80 rupees for this chair? Loot liya tujhe toh. Re bawle, 40 ka toh yahin gaon mein ban jaati. Luta bhi, aur dhukhi hua who alag…" Saying this, he carried on. (You have been robbed, stupid. You could have gotten a chair made right here in the village for forty rupees. You got robbed, and took so much pains of travel over it too.)

Gopi had covered some distance when he came across another farmer, Subey. After exchanging pleasantries, Subey asked him the same question as Jilley.

"E—" Gopi stopped before he could complete the number, remembering the ridicule he had just faced on saying eighty. He genuinely believed that he had made a mistake by paying double the amount. 'Eaaah, forty rupees,' he finally said.

"Forty? What is so special about this chair that you paid so much? Could have bought one of the same quality here itself in the village for twenty rupees. It would have saved you the bus fare too."

This got Gopi thinking again, 'Is it possible that I could have made such a big mistake? Twenty rupees and the same quality? Sattey carpenter is not bad, but could he have delivered this quality? I seriously doubt it.' As he was evaluating all this, he saw another neighbour coming by. Again, he was not looking at him, but at the chair on his head.

It looked solid and built with good wood. "Shesham, han?" he asked. "How much did you pay for it?" Gopi had already made a fool of himself twice by quoting a high price, and Subey had just told him that its value was not more than twenty rupees, so Gopi told this person that it was for twenty rupees.

"The chair doesn't look bad, but if you ask me frankly, twenty is a high price you paid. I am sure you could have managed to get it made here for ten," said the neighbour.

Another hundred yards and he would be home, but he was so upset by this time that he felt like throwing the chair away in a corner and return to his sugarcane fields. 'The crop will be good this year, it'll calm me down,' thought he as he entered his street and came face to face with his old friend – Jaggu.

"Bara jaldi mein hai, Gopi, kya hua? Kursi le he aaya, kitne mein pari?" he asked. (Why are you in such a hurry, Gopi? What happened? I see, you finally bought a chair. How much did you pay for it?)

Gopi was so upset by this time that he simply said, "I got it for free, as I paid in kind by taking my pants down."

This is what happens when we are not confident or not able to take criticism.

Things to live by:

a. Compete with the self, not others

b. Be original

c. Balance out

There are so many things around us, so many distractions, that we feel lost at times. *Where to go? What to do? How to start?* We start looking to others for guidance. In this process, we lose our originality and start copying others or listening to others. We don't realise that nobody can know us like we know ourselves. For acceptance in our families and the society, we suppress and hide our real selves, fearing that our chosen path might be ridiculed, our larger than life goals may be laughed at, and our decisions may not be supported. This results in a loss of confidence in ourselves and our decisions. We have to believe in ourselves to attain our goals.

You can achieve your larger than life goals only by being original...

"At times, the best answer to a question is another question."

4.6 Courage works in our favour, not truth.

It was in one of the lectures during class 11th that Jacob, the school peon with twirling moustaches, appeared at the classroom door and informed our teacher that roll number 1973 had been summoned by the headmaster immediately. This meant only one thing – BIG TROUBLE. Physical beatings back then were not only common, but almost an everyday affair, specially since it was a Sainik School, run by the Ministry of Defence, and we had to be trained in resilience in preparation of becoming Armed Forces' officers.

With a thumping heart and a dry throat I reached the Headmaster's office. There, I found another roommate standing, facing the wall. He was popular by his nickname 'boxer'. Only by the movement of my eyes, I asked him what this was all about, as I had no idea at all. He made a gesture with his hands which meant – *we are screwed.*

I was asked to stand apart from boxer, facing another wall. Muffled sounds of beatings from inside the office made me even more tense, and my brain ran in all directions to recall any hint of misgiving from the last few days, but nothing, nada.

Shortly, it was my turn to face the demon. I knocked on the door and stuttered, "May I come in, sir?" I wanted this ordeal be over and quickly. I heard the sound of approval and walked in, steeling my body and bracing it for all the slaps, punches and cane beatings coming its way. The headmaster looked at me for a few seconds without saying anything. His gaze was intense and it appeared as if he was enjoying every moment before jumping for the kill.

"So Ramesh, you are fond of dancing, isn't it?" It was hard to believe what I had just heard. It could be a trap, I realized and kept mum. "You dance with your roommates and other friends, but naked–all of you, and late at night too." Then I remembered that it had happened just once and a couple of months back. A roommate had smuggled in a stereo and somebody had planned this dance just for the heck of it. But who could snitch, I wondered, it was taken very seriously.

"Sir, we danced once some months ago, but with our underwear on as it was particularly hot that day."

"You bugger, you are telling a lie!" A tight slap came next. My skin burned with the impact. I was in a dilemma. I couldn't tell him the entire truth, especially the names of others involved. I had no idea how much the Headmaster knew.

"Okay, now think hard before telling me, did you try to force yourself upon someone?" Another hard slap came before I could even complete saying no.

"You want to play games now? Fine, games we shall play."

"But sir, I am telling the truth!" This time, a strong kick knocked against my shins. "Go, be a cock in that corner," he said and pointed to his left.

Within five minutes, my legs started trembling and beads of sweat dripped down to the floor. I shifted my weight from one leg to the other to give myself some temporary relief. Every little movement of mine was rewarded with a kick. It was becoming unbearable, but there was no relief in sight. I was about to give up when I received another kick and a command to get up. It took me a few seconds to stand up straight, My face was red and my shirt drenched. The headmaster supported himself against the edge of the table and asked again, "Did you try to rape someone?"

"No sir," I repeated. "Sir, please at least tell me who is accusing me of it? Let him face me directly and say the same thing to my face. It is not true."

He dismissed me with a warning, "You will not discuss anything of what happened today with anyone, do you get it? Anyone! I will call for you later."

It became somewhat clear later that day when boxer shared that the Headmaster had asked him if three of us roommates had tried to rape 'Baingan'. (Brinjal)

"What?" I almost jumped. "Who the heck would want to even think about such an ugly person."

"Exactly, this is what I told the headmaster. *Sir, please take a look at Narayan and ask me the same question again.* If at all one were to think of screwing somebody, it would be a junior with a round plump ass and a smooth skin; no resistance from the other end and enjoyment from our end. Who would think of even looking at this ape?" That justification probably saved us.

It was much later when we found out that Narayan's father had wanted to get him out of Sainik school and get a clerical job. Since the government paid the scholarship of students at Sainik Schools, one was not allowed to leave the school before appearing for the NDA exams. In such a case, a full scholarship amount was supposed to be paid back by the parents as compensation. A wicked teacher had given Narayan's father the idea of accusing his roommates of sexual harassment to get him out without paying a single penny.

Many years later, I asked that teacher what kick he got out of ruining innocent students' lives.He looked at me as if I had spoiled his evening.

Things not to live by:

a. Meanness

b. Violence

c. Oppression

We do not win by being naïve against adversaries that are mean, violent and oppressive. We have to be street-smart to win. A lot of times, we come across people who are completely different than us. Everybody doesn't have the same principles, or has only a single principle of torturing the weak. You may be weaker in strength or position, but if you are strong psychologically, you can turn their own strength against them by playing with their mind instead of attacking directly, in which case you may lose.

Your strength lies in not only understanding yourself but also the psyche of your opponent...

Chapter 5

Perceptions

"If you are in the business of judging, you have chosen the worst possible one."

5.1 Bicycle and Judging:

This happened in mid-1960s, in one of the villages in Rohtak, Haryana.

Ramphal, a farmer, had to visit one of his close relatives in a neighbouring village. The news was not good. He had to hurry.

The best and the quickest way to reach there was by borrowing his friend Kirshen's bicycle, he thought. He started towards his friend's house which was at the other end of the village. He had hardly walked a hundred steps when he came across his neighbour, Fattey. After some initial greetings, Fattey asked him where he was off to. Ramphal told him about the news from his relatives and his plan to borrow his friend Kirshen's bicycle.

Fattey looked at him as if Ramphal was not in his right mind. "Why would Kirshen lend his bicycle to you?" he asked. "You know that a bicycle is not so common a thing. There are only two in our entire village."

"Why would he not lend it to me?" asked Ramphal. "We are childhood friends. We have helped each other through thick and thin."

"So what?" Fattey said. "If you have helped him, he has helped you too. Isn't it? That is a different matter, but a bicycle is something precious. Anyway, it is upto you if you want to make a fool out of yourself. If I were in your place, I would never even think about it. *Chalo bhai, theek hai, mein chalta hoon,"* said Fattey and went his way. (Okay then, brother, I'll take your leave.)

Ramphal stood there for a few moments, thinking what to do. He was confused now and started thinking, 'How is it possible that Kirshen will refuse? Didn't I carry his sick son on my shoulders to the doctor when Kirshen was away? Didn't I make available myself for three days and nights for his daughter's marriage? How could he forget that?' Only the next moment, he recalled how Kirshen has helped him when his mother was not well. He had taken her to the civil hospital and had even stayed there for four whole days till she recovered.

'Is a bicycle more important than a friend? How could Kirshen even think that way? This is completely wrong. If this is indeed what he thinks, I'll take him to task. Someone should open his eyes,' he made up his mind and resumed his walk to confront his friend. The more he thought about it, the more he felt certain that his friend was completely in the wrong. 'How could he forget that I have even lied for him, the very first lie of my adulthood. Maybe he is no longer the Krishen I once knew. He has a bicycle, perhaps that is why he thinks he is better than I am. He does own more land and got his daughter married into a wealthy family. Perhaps all this has gone to his head.' Such thoughts keep on invading his mind as he neared his friend's house.

By the time he reached Kirshen's house, he felt terribly angry and wronged already. He kicked open the door and shouted for his friend. Kirshen came out and smiled upon seeing his friend. "Welcome Ramphal, my brother. Long time, han? I thought you have forgotten your old friend. Tell me, what brings you here?"

Ramphal retorted, "bhool toh tu gaya. Apne cycle ka itna ghamand? Nahin chahiye tera cycle" ("You're the one who has forgotten. So much pride for a single bicycle? I don't need your bicycle.")

Kirshan was confused for his friend's anger. "Who told you that? Cycle chahiye naa, le ja bhai" ("Who told you that? If you need my bicycle, you can of course take it.")

"Arey, nahin chahiye, tera cycle; mein toh paidal he kaam chala loonga; rakh apna cycle apne pichwade mein" ("I said I don't need it. Take it and shove it up your rear end. I will manage on foot,") … and saying this Rampahl walked away, leaving his friend even more confused.

When we judge people,

a. We lose opportunities

b. We become more negative, which can become a habit

c. It lowers our acceptance, and hence the happiness in our lives

We judge people too soon; this is how our mind works. To keep things simple, our mind separates all things into good or bad, like or dislike, trust or distrust, safe or dangerous. Social scientists say that we take just about nine seconds to form an opinion about others. If I cannot claim to know myself completely, how can I claim to know somebody else in just a few seconds? By forming prejudices, we lose on the opportunities to form long lasting relationships, we lose business opportunities, we become negative in our approach and are less happy. Instead, let us take things on as they come with an open mind.

If we look at things/people as they are, there will always be a lot to learn and gain.

"If you want to walk with someone, wear the same shoes as them."

5.2 Guru ji and 'gur':

A father was very concerned about his young son who was extremely fond of 'gur', and had tried in vain to make him let go of this habit. His cajoling, putting fear in his mind, and even threatening made no difference to his craving for 'gur'.

'Let me take him to Guruji,' the father thought. 'He has solved the problems of so many people.'

The next evening, he took his son to the Guruji. After the initial pleasantries, he told him the problem. Guruji smiled and said, "No problem, come back in three days and I'll speak to him." The father touched Guruji's feet, took his blessings and left happy.

When they returned three days later, the Guruji received them with kindness, but asked then to visit again in two days. When they did so, they were again told to come back after a couple of days.

On the said day, the Guruji was ready to receive them. He told the father to wait outside as he would speak to his son in private.

Guruji asked the kid why he liked 'gur' so much.

"I don't know for sure," the kid replied. "I just like how it tastes."

"And do you know what harm it does if you take it in excess quantity?" he asked, then went on to gradually explaining all possible problems that he would face, what it would mean for his physical health, and how it would disturb his psychological wellbeing as well if he continued his habit of consuming 'gur'. He gave the kid a few examples and also advised him on what to do when he craved for it. The kid listened attentively and promised to do as he was told.

The father was then called and told that there was nothing to worry now as his son had understood the consequences of this bad habit, and had promised to leave it. The father thanked his Guru profusely and left with his son. Once outside, he asked his son to wait and went back in to ask Guruji one last question.

"Guruji, there is something that is baffling me. Why did you postpone this meeting three times? You are wise and you could have said the same wise things to my son all these days ago to convince him to kick this habit."

Guruji smiled and said, "Son, the truth is that I was very fond of gur too. Initially, I thought that I could kick this habit in a couple of days, but I couldn't and it took me more time than I had thought. I was finally able to do it two days ago, and only then was I ready to convince your son. How could I have convinced someone to let go of a bad habit if I was guilty of it myself?"

Discipline your mind

a. Observe your thoughts (both positive and negative) and write them down

b. Reward yourself for positive thoughts, and keep adding to the good habits

c. Exercise and meditate

We are good at giving 'gyan'. Teachers, parents, bosses, neighbours, relatives — all have something to share – their perception of things. But how many of these 'gyan gurus' actually practise what they preach? We should look at actions and not words to accept the teachings of someone, besides its relevance to our goals. We should also think deep at the motivation behind such a discourse.

Never believe a person if his/her words and actions do not match.

"Having more doesn't bring peace of mind, it only brings more hunger."

5.3 Majuli – fishing and clarity of goal:

Majuli is the largest river island in the world, down Brahmaputra in upper Assam. This story is about a native fisherman there.

Early one morning, a fisherman was out in Majuli to catch his daily quota of fish. He was middle aged and heavy in the middle. He removed some wet sand at the river bank to fit in his stomach and lied down to start catching his fish. Soon, he was joined by an educated looking young man who was also carrying a fishing rod. The young man smiled at the other person, took out his folding chair and sat on it to start his day.

The young man was curious about how the other person could be so at peace with himself.

The middle aged person was also curious about the seriousness of the young. He asked the young man what his plan was for the day.

"Well, I'll catch as many fish as possible," he answered.

"And then what?"

"This. I would continue till I save up enough money for a fish net."

"And after that?" the middle-aged man asked.

"Then, I'll be able catch more fish and save more money for a fishing boat."

"That sounds good," the other person said. "And what after that?"

"After that, I'll employ a couple of people to catch more fish for me."

"Will you be happy then?"

"No," the young man replied. "After that, I'll buy a fish trawler so that I can employ more people to catch more fish."

The middle-aged man was contemplating what the young man would do then, when he, as if reading the man's thoughts, went on, "I will buy a warehouse next to store my fish and supply them to other areas of the country. After that, I will start exporting to other countries as well."

"And what after that?" the middle-aged person asked.

"Then, I'll become rich and enjoy my life."

"Oh! All this to enjoy your life? What do you think I am doing right now?"

Peace is a state of mind.

How to achieve peace of mind?

a. Draw a line between necessity and desire

b. Find time for people and things you love

c. Develop a habit of sharing time, knowledge and money

When we are young, we may have time and energy, but no money; in middle age, we may have energy and money, but no time; in old age, we may have time and money, but no energy. How can one strike a balance between these three to achieve peace of mind? The youth can invest their time and energy in education and learning; the middle aged can invest their energy and money into their future, and the old can give something back to the society with their time and resources. If we only work for money, we shall lose our family/friends and hamper self-development. The sooner we realize it, the better.

Understand the difference between necessities and desires; develop meaningful relations and develop a habit of giving back to the society.

"Don't start a fire when there is no water around."

5.4 One round in the chamber:

I was sharing a two-room set with a friend in Sector 6 Panchkula, a posh area, in the early nineties. Once, he had a couple of unusual visitors over – leaders of a kidnapping gang wanted by the police of five states. Just out of college, those were my carefree days and I didn't think much about the precarious situation I could be in by having them as my house guests.

They were carrying a 9mm pistol and I asked them to show me how it worked. I was told that it makes a very loud noise. I asked, "Why don't you carry a more silent weapon then?"

"Because our job is not to kill anyone, and when fired, its sound would put fear into people's minds, that's all we want," they told me.

It was my birthday, 9th August, and I had planned to go out with a friend for a couple of beers and lunch at Pinjore Garden restaurant. That friend got delayed in coming to my house, and waiting had always been a problem with me. I opened the guest's suitcase, pulled out the pistol, and removed its magazine as was shown to me the previous day. 'Now it is safe to play with,' I thought and started examining it closely. The trigger was hard to press and I thought it might be locked where the magazine was connected. I was trying to figure out its mechanism while a finger was still on the trigger, and **BOOM!**

It was a loud sound, very loud. I stood frozen for a few seconds and tried to find out where the bullet had hit. Then I saw it, a hole just above the bed on the wall. With my heart thumping against my rib cage, I tried to look for the spent bullet. It looked like a thick shirt button lying on the floor. I picked it up, put in my trousers' pocket and thought of running away as far as possible. The sound had been quite different from what one hears in the movies. An average person could not have recognised it, but there were two Army officers clubs and a police officers' club within the aerial distance of 70-80 meters from my house and I was afraid they might have heard it.

My hands were trembling and heart was pumping fast and loud. I knew it could turn out to be the worst incident of my life. Guilty or not guilty, there was no bail under TADA, no open court either. I was certainly done for life.

My first thought was to run away, still unsure of whether I should carry the gun with me or to throw it away. I realized the next moment that just a couple of days back, some senior government official had been shot dead in the very same area, and the Haryana government had created a post of SP at Panchkula (till then DSP was in charge of that area). Everywhere, police check posts had come up and every vehicle was being checked. 'Damn it, what if I carry this pistol and am stopped for checking?' I thought. 'My face is certain to give me away the moment I am stopped.' I looked back at the small crater the bullet had left in the wall, and covered it with a pillow. I couldn't think of much else and there was no time.

I turned to go out, then stopped, thought for the best place to hide the gun, couldn't think of a better place than the same suitcase it had come out from, and thought once again but my brain was going crazy and was not of much help. I took out the bullet shell from my trousers' pocket and put it in my socks to be thrown away later.

Luckily, I was not stopped at any police check-post anywhere on my way to my friend's place. His looked at me and his face changed to a frown from a smile. "What the hell happened? You look as white as a ghost." He looked at me closely from my toes to my head and asked, "Are you hurt? Was there an accident?"

"A glass of water," was all I could say. I gulped down a glassful, then took a deep breath as it was not helping to get my overzealous heart under control. Once I had calmed down a bit, I told him everything.

"What do you want to do now?" my friend asked.

"I am sure police would be crawling around the place now. I want to assess their reaction, but from a safe distance. Rest depends on the ground situation. I want you to give me a ride back as I am not certain about my abilities under this extreme pressure."

"Fine," replied the friend and started his bike.

Initially, we rode very slowly past the rear street, then turned and stopped at the farthest corner. Observing the area very attentively, I took out a cigarette and lit it. The bike's engine was still on. Fear still had complete control over me. After watching for around five minutes, we drove off. We returned again after fifteen odd minutes to look for any subtle activity, but it still looked peaceful — so far so good.

It was time to find the owners of the unwanted product and tell them about the incident. They started back from Chandigarh, slowing down before every traffic signal or speeding up as they did not want to be trapped between other vehicles in case they had to run. After all, police force from five states was looking for them. They also took some time looking for any tell-tale signs outside the house. When satisfied, they entered the house, took their suitcase, and were gone. It was then that I finally heaved a sigh of great relief.

Later on, I was told that they never stayed at one place for a long time. They changed vehicles very frequently and always dry-cleaned their clothes. First two I could understand – third, I never could.

Whom to trust?

a. Avoid acting on impulse

b. Avoid hard sellers

c. Look at their credibility, motives and actions

Take time to trust someone; impulsive trust comes with a price. Trust starts with small matters and builds over time with positive outcome each & every time. We either trust someone or not, it can't be 50% or even 99%. Trusting someone is equivalent to taking risks as we are depending on the other person. More often than not, we don't know how we would react to certain situations or people. Taking risks till we are self-aware and can manage the self well should be limited to what we can afford. Before taking such actions, we need to think through to the consequences of our risky actions and decide whether we can bear to live with those consequences or not.

Before trusting ourselves, we have to know ourselves.

"Truth changes with the perception."

5.5 Poor and Rich – perception:

In nineteenth century, a poor young man called Sattu was in the market to sell his wares. As common in those days, markets were held weekly at a centrally located place alongside a road, so that citizens from the neighbouring areas could gather to buy things. Sattu was bargaining with a customer who was walking away. At that moment, a rich and influential person was passing through that crowded road.

This person was on a *bughi* (carriage) with two *laithats* (bodyguards) standing at the front of the *bughi* to clear any obstruction in the way. "What are you looking at, you fools?" the rich man shouted. "Do I pay you to just look at things or make way for me? Get your arses down and cane these lazy bastards who are blocking the road."

The bodyguards started caning the people on the road and it was clear in no time. Sattu also suffered some canes on his back, and scurried back to his temporary stall. He looked up at heaven and said, "God, why did you send these rich snobs to Earth. Was it to beat up poor people like me? I would never do that if I ever become as successful as that man."

Time passed and a few years later, Sattu became a successful businessman. He was well respected in his town. He now owned a *bughi* and his own two *laithats* stood in front of it whenever he travelled for business.

One day, they came across a congested road-side market. He was tired and getting late for home. He looked at his *laithats* and ordered them to make way immediately. The *laithats* got down and started canning the people blocking the road. On watching the poor people getting canned, Sattu looked towards heaven and said, "God, why do you send these poor wretches to Earth, to get canned?"

This is how our perception changes with time.

Expectations:

a. We always look at the world as an extension of our own selves

b. The speed of change in us is different from the speed of change at large

c. With power comes a changed outlook

We always look at the world as an extension of our own selves. If you trust the people around, you also expect them to trust you; if you are a truth speaker, you expect other people to speak the truth to you as well. When you are poor, you don't trust the rich; and when you are rich, you trust no one – this is how our expectations work. At times, we meet people after a long period and don't see any of the things in them that we had known them for. We find them changed faster than us or our expectations.

Change is inevitable, but if we change our core values, we may one day find ourselves to be that which we once hated.

"Past is just like ash; you can't cook your meal on it."

5.6 Only past:

I once joined a new company and didn't know much about it. As was customary, I was invited to the 'bura Bungalow' (Manager's Bungalow) along with my family members for dinner. I had a good discussion with my boss. He told me a lot about the glorious past of our company. "You know, our company was a pioneer in Tea. We initiated forming the Tea Association, and we have contributed handsomely for various CSR programs. Also, just after independence, RBI Kolkata branch once borrowed from us. Our company is so great that the return cheque from RBI was never encashed, but was put in a frame. It is still on the wall of our Chairman's office."

The evening was great. I felt so proud to be a part of such a great organization, but something was missing – what was it?

It was the next day when sitting with another colleague, I realized what it was that had been missing from the conversation the evening before. "How was the meeting with the old man yesterday?" my colleague asked me in a guarded way.

"It went very well," I said. "but can I share something with you with an understanding that you will not quote me on this?"

He hesitated, then said, "Sure, it will stay between us."

"I think this company doesn't have a great future."

"Why do you say so?" he asked.

"Because for the entire evening yesterday, boss shared a lot of great things about this company from the past, but never spoke about any future plans. If a company's future is bright, one would talk about its growth plans, expansions, acquisitions, adding new business verticals, etc. and not just about what happened in the past."

The colleague just smiled and said, "You would find out soon where we stand."

And I did. I wish I would have been wrong.

Emotions versus Logic

a. Emotional decisions are not good for the long term

b. Decisions based on cold hard logic are at times not humane

c. Seek a wise balance between both – right decisions without sacrificing the humaneness

We should avoid buying things sold emotionaly. Every one of us is a salesperson; as children, we sell our need for love and toys, as adolescents for more freedom, and as grown-ups our beliefs and values. We either use emotions or logic to sell something. In an interview, a candidate sells his knowledge and skills, and the interviewer his/her organization. The problem arises when we exchange the use of emotions for logic and vice versa, in which case, the result may not be as per our expectations.

Striking a balance between emotions and logic may get us some peace at the end of the day.

"Picking a battle wisely can win you a war."

5.7 Army at 'gherao':

In 2002, I was posted at a tea estate near Tinsukia and was looking after the manufacturing. On a Monday just after noon, estate workers started gathering in front of the office and within half an hour, more than a thousand had gathered. When I reached the office, it was already a chaos there — shouting, slogans and angry red faces all around. I asked my colleagues what had happened and was told that the workers were looking for Jamal who had irked the women by not allowing them to cross a waist-deep river by boats, for which reason they had to cross the river by pulling up their sarees.

I tried to speak to the workers' leaders, but nobody was ready to listen. "Sahib, just hand over Jamal sahib to us. He has hidden himself somewhere in the office." I knew that that was not a possibility as incidents like this could lead to fatal consequences. An angry crowd has no bounds, and in situations like that humanity is the first causality, just as in a war.

"Theek hai, aap log kaam pe jao. Javed sahib ne kuch galat kiya hai toh jaroor kaarwahi hogi, aur aap kal aake unse mil sakte hain," I tried to pacify them. (Okay, I have heard you. Please go back to your work. If Jamal sahib has done something wrong, appropriate action will be taken. You can come back tomorrow to meet him).

But that was not to happen. They wanted him then and there, and we could not let that happen. We prepared ourselves for a long 'gherao'. Gherao is very common in the tea industry where workers encircle you for hours and you cannot go out of that circle for even drinking water, using the loo or for meals. The workers, however, keep slipping for homemade liquor in batches of 30-40, and come fully charged for shouting abuses, slogans, and at times start violence too. Also, the tea estates have around 50% of women workforce and during a 'gherao', they make the first ring around you so there is no way out. If you touch them in any way to go out, you are as good as dead.

We were hoping to persuade the workers to return to their work and knew that it would cool their tempers down, but none of them was ready to listen to anything or anyone.

After a couple of hours, I told the crowd to let me out of the circle to look for Jamal, and called the police station to inform them of the deteriorating situation at the estate. It was the peak of insurgency and even the police vehicles didn't venture out without the support of CRPF, and took time to reach.

Before the police, there came four army men with assault rifles. They were from the Army company stationed in our estate, as it was a sensitive area in terms of insurgency. I knew most of them and they knew me. I heaved a sigh of relief at their sight. I felt sure that nobody would get hurt that day. It was the Jat regiment and the JCO leading them was at least 6'5" tall. The workers made way for them to enter the circle as they wanted to speak to me.

"*Kundu sa'ab, apne CO saab se message aaya hai aapko yahan se nikalene ke liye. Aap hamare saath chalo,*" one of them said. (We have been asked by our commanding officer to take you out from here, please come with us.) That was unthinkable, so I thanked him for his concern and asked him to convey my thanks to the

CO as well. "Sa'ab, this situation is not good and I cannot leave till it is sorted out."

"Par sa'ab, hamare CO saab ka huqam hai toh aapko saath le ke jaayenge," he said and looked at the crowd with fervor in his eyes, as if challenging the crowd to try stopping him from carrying out his CO's order. (It is our CO's order and we shall not leave till it is fulfilled.)

One of the workers in the front turned back and shouted, *"Aaj yahan se koi nahin jayega, kisi ko nahin jaane denge jab tak who kutta Jamal humen nahin mil jata."*(Nobody can leave this place today till we get our hands on that dog Jamal.) This irked the JCO and he pushed the worker back with his cane, inviting more shouting, slogans, and abuses towards the Army. The two soldiers cocked their weapons at them. It was getting worse by the moment.

I turned to the JCO and said slowly with utmost certainty, *"Sa'ab, ye saare mere workers hain aur inhen takleef hai isi liye yahan khaana-peena chhorkar mere paas aaye hain. Ye ghar ka maamla hai, ise hum ghar mein he apne tarike se suljhaa lege, aapka phir se dhanyavaad par aap ja sakte hain."* (These are my workers and they are here because they have a problem. It is an internal matter of our family and we will sort it out as family members. Thank you for your concern, but please carry on.) I tried to hug the JCO so that I could indicate to him with a very slight push that he should go back. My arms were just above his belt. He looked down at me for a few moments, but said nothing. He pulled out his walkie talkie and informed his company commander that they were pulling out.

The workers were even more vehement now. It was around 5 PM, and soon to get dark. I was worried because certain segment of workers would take advantage of darkness for instigating violence. More abuses, shouting and chaos followed. The police arrived at around 5.45 PM along with the CRPF personnel, but the workers had already become violent by then. The police people tried to talk to the workers, but in vain. They assessed the situation, then pulled all the executives into the office. Stone pelting started soon after. One CRPF person tried to aim his rifle at them, but I ran to him and told him not to fire.

They managed to break most of window glasses, but the crowd started thinning out after that. It had been a close shave.

The next day, I visited the Army camp, but the JCO was not happy. *"Ye toh aap the sa'ab, nahin toh koi hamari vardi ko chhoo nahin sakta, aur hum CRPF se nahin hain jo ghutne pe goli maarte hain, hum toh seedha senay pe maarte,"* he stated matter of fact. (We stopped because of you, sir. Otherwise, you know nobody can touch our uniform. We are not like those CRPF men who aim at the knees. We would have aimed straight at their chest.)

"Tabhi toh aapko waapas bhej diya tha, kyonki mujhe pata tha ke kal naa aap peeche hattey aur naa workers," I replied. (That's why I sent you back yesterday, as I knew very well that neither you nor my workers would have taken a step back yesterday.)

I stayed on that estate for a couple more years and had a beautiful time as I had won the workers' complete trust.

Trust comes with a sacrifice of personal gains.

'Risk' versus 'no risk' versus 'calculated risk'

a. Total risk may cause you to lose everything
b. No risk may cause you to not achieve your goals
c. Calculated risk may aid you in growth without sacrificing a better future

Some people will jump into a raging fire, while some hesitate to touch a warm candle, yet there are others who are choosy in playing with fire. Our disposition in this regard depends on two things – our risk taking capacity and the circumstances. At times, the risk takers may jump into the fire to save their loved ones, but won't endanger their lives to save their burning house. It also depends upon whether we value safety shell more or venture out to build relationships for long term. We can either sacrifice our today to build a secure tomorrow, or be short sighted and enjoy what we have today rather than work for an uncertain future.

A short term sacrifice may be necessary to build a long term relationship.

"Fear only fears knowledge."

5.8 The Police Station

There are certain unwritten rules in families, organizations and societies which are more important than even the written ones.

In the late eighties in my college in Chandigarh, we were on a strike as our college authorities were taking the Punjab problem as an excuse for not holding the student body elections. Elections for the Parliament and the State Assembly were being held, but not in educational institutions. On a Friday afternoon, sixteen of us were picked up by the police and were taken to the police station. The courts were to open on Monday morning, and we had three nights to spend there as state guests. It was a unique learning experience for us.

The first evening when the policemen came back to the Police Station for depositing their firearms, they were tired but still looking for fun — if one were to consider beating someone mercilessly as fun.

Out of experience, they knew who to speak to in a hard tone, who to slap and who to kick. Thieves and harassment culprits were for kicking, petty quarrel participants were for slaps, and people like us who looked somewhat confident were for harsh words only.

One person was locked in under a rape accusation. We watched him getting the third degree treatment first hand. He was made to sprawl face-down on the floor. A policeman pinned down his stretched out hands by his feet, another had his legs under control, and a third one had a wide wet leather strip with "*aan milo sajna*" written on it. It was used to strike the rapist's legs and buttocks. It left welts and ugly blue sores on his body. He was held by a policeman by his hair and was made to run in the gallery to make blood circulation normal again as welts restrict the blood circulation. It was difficult for him initially to follow their commands, which invited more strikes and kicks. After he became normal, the treatment was repeated, and this continued for quite a few times till he could take no more. This is not to even mention the abusive words which followed consistently.

Watching all this first hand made us realize a couple of things. First, the police worked on a strict hierarchy, and second, the punishment is as per the policemen's perception of the crime that one has committed.

One good outcome of this experience was that our fear of the police vanished completely.

Open to learning

a. You learn to gain knowledge, which in turn helps you to make better decisions in present

b. Change is the only constant thing – learning will keep you relevant for tomorrow

c. Learning helps us in developing others – which leads to a better family/organization/society

Every situation teaches you something, provided you are open for learning. The toughest situations bring out your hidden talents, even you were not aware of. It is the fear which stops us from taking chances as we think it is safer for us not to do anything; for learning and growth–we have to face our fear and overcome it. Most of the animals – from dogs to snakes attack when they either fear for their life or smell fear in us; the moment we control our fear and don't react, the chances of being attacked become minimal.

Adverse situations are our best teachers...

Chapter 6

Fight Your Way Out

"Faith and fear are opposites. Faith dilutes fear and fear weakens faith."

6.1 Faith vs. Fear

A person in old clothes which needed washing approached Jaggu, a friend, at his house in Panchkula with a request to get him a job of a gardener. It was mid-nineties and Jaggu had good political connections. Since the person had not come through a direct source, the situation demanded that Jaggu speaks to him well, offers him a cup of tea, and promises to look into the matter. He had no intention of getting the job done. Jaggu asked him to get in touch again.

The job of a gardener in schools was considered a stress free one in which one didn't need to work hard. It was a sought after job by unskilled people. The other option was being a peon, but a peon's job was below status for higher casts, and was a hard work in addition to being ordered about by everyone else in school.

After about four years, Jaggu was once going out to office late in the morning when a Tata Sumo stopped in front of his house and a person in a spotless white kurta pajama (white overalls) got down and greeted him, "Bhai saab pahchana? (Did you recognise me, sir?) I am so and so and had approached you for a government gardener's job around four years back." He was a bundle of energy. Jaggu, of course, didn't recognise him, but smiled, "Of course, I have recognized you. How are you? And how is everyone else in the family? Come, let's have a cup of tea. We can talk during that period, as I have to rush out immediately after that."

"Tell me, what I can do for you?" Jaggu asked as soon as they sat down for a cup of tea.

"Actually, I came to know that some shop cum office plots are being auctioned by HUDA (Haryana Urban Development Authority) in Panchkula. I don't know the process but thought of you as one person who can help me in buying a couple. I am thinking of constructing showrooms as that would be a good permanent income for me and even for my kids," he said.

Jaggu looked at him closely without appearing to be offensive. He could not think of anything which would transform a person's financial situation from receiving a salary of a couple of thousand rupees to being able to buy a couple of crores properties. 'What the hell did he do? It must be a mistake, as he has no idea how much these SCOs cost,' he thought.

"Yes, I know that SCOs are being auctioned next week, and can help you there. I know somebody in HUDA and will connect you to him. But you know the cost of these plots. One would cost you around a crore," said Jaggu.

"Yes, bhai saab, I have an idea and want to buy a couple," said the man.

Without being impolite, Jaggu asked him indirectly what he was doing and how it was going.

"Oh, it is going great. I get alcohol from Rajasthan and sell it at a good profit at the Haryana border. (Bansi Lal had promised to make Haryana a dry state, and after he became CM in 1996, he declared it as one.) Initially, I used to carry in small quantities, but then I started using jeeps, and lately, it is coming in by truckloads. People need to forget their worries at the end of the day, and somebody had to provide this service. There is a lot of demand, and thus a lot of profit in it as well. It is run smoothly in a systematic way, sir. All concerned are involved in it," he responded.

Faith versus Fear:

a. A strong faith dilutes fear

b. A strong fear weakens faith

c. An opportunity always lies beyond our fear

Fear is comparative. Only fools or mentally challenged can afford to be fearless in absolute terms. It depends on our take on life and circumstances, but faith in something alleviates fear - even if it is faith in a corrupt system. Letting go of an opportunity most times is connected to our fear - fear of law, society, failure or the unknown. If your or your family's financial security is the larger goal, then fear takes a backseat. The rewards depend on the chances we take. Larger the chances, bigger are the rewards. It is an individual's choice whether to take chances in life or live a stress free life — each one comes at a cost. Taking chances may convert your dreams into reality, but with a pitfall of standing against the law. Having peace of mind, on the other hand, brings serenity, but you may have to let go of your dreams. If you get both, then consider yourself a lucky exception.

To alleviate fear, put a larger goal in front of you.

"Lose a battle, win a war."

6.2 Karan Singh and office files:

In the Tea industry, most of our bosses were trained under expats, mostly Irish, who left in the late seventies after FERA changes during Indira Gandhi's government. These managers had a very different style of management – hard working, harder partying, not caring for others' opinions, taking full responsibility for everything happening under their watch, and never blaming their team members.

An estate manager in Tea functions more or less like a CO (Commanding Officer) of infantry regiments in the Army, but has much more independence with regard to making decisions. An estate manager is a one man show who looks after the field as well as the manufacturing operations, finance and budgeting, marketing and sales, industrial relations, mechanical and civil engineering, medicine, liaisons, and so enjoys almost absolute power of decision making.

Mr. Karan Singh got promoted as Director and joined at the Calcutta Head Office. He was given the advice to understand the culture first as it was completely opposite to his 'bagaan' culture. "The pace and style of working in the left ruled Calcutta will need a lot of patience from your end," he was told repeatedly.

"Don't worry," he replied, "I have been visiting this office for the last 30 odd years. I know how it works here."

One day, he called his peon and someone else walked in. "*Aapnar peon chutti te achhey, babu, uder sharir bhal nahin*. Tell me, what is it that you want?" he asked. (Your peon is on leave, sir, he is not well.)

Karan didn't like the casual manner in which he was being spoken to, but remembered the advice given to him. He said, "I need the budget file on Dhula tea estate, hurry up."

"It was handled by your peon. He only knows where he has kept it. Let him come back," came the reply.

"But he is sick, he may take a week or even more. I can't wait for so long. Go and find it." The person in front of him didn't move.

"Fine, I'll go and find it myself. Just tell me where these files are kept." Karan got up and walked out of his office. He stopped outside, still waiting to get the directions to the room where he could find that file. The other person called a couple of employees and told them what 'babu' was looking for. One of them came forward and told him, "Sir, *itta hovey naa*." (You can't look for the file, and neither would any of us.)

"But why?"

"It is your peon's job to bring it to you, and if you find it today, you may say tomorrow that you don't require him anymore. Nobody is going to lose his job if you just wait for him to come back, so wait."

"No, no, you don't understand, it is urgent. And he won't lose his job, I give you my word on it," Karan explained.

"Sorry sir, the file will have to wait and this is how it works here. Please go back to your office if you don't want a strike." Perplexed and totally at a loss for words the first time, he just kept looking on till they returned to their usual work.

Unlearn to learn

Change the mapping,

1. Adapt to new realities
2. Evolve with time
3. Change what you can; accept what you can't

Adapting to a new environment is a skill most of us have to acquire, as only some are born with this ability. Understanding the culture to which we have transported ourselves is the first step to prepare ourselves for this change. If we want to bring about some change, the first step is to win the trust of people around us. When people know you and your intentions, only then do you find support in them for that change. Communicating to them the need for a change and their own benefit in it makes it a lot easier.

Win other's trust before you start working on a change.

"If you can't accept something; change it."

6.3 A walk late at night:

With a couple of friends I had gone to watch an evening show of a movie in Chandigarh. After the show we were walking back to our hostel at around 9.30 PM. It was during summers and it was fairly hot even that late in the night. Some couples were strolling on the road inside the colony. Around 15-20 yards in front of us, five students were walking along shouting, laughing, jumping and abusing each other as well as Om Puri – lead actor of the movie we had just watched, and who happened to be one of my favourite actors. I had liked the movie; it was different. With every passing minute, I was getting more angry at their boisterousness which was disturbing others around them.

"What is your problem, Kundu? Why get so stressed? Either accept it or change it," said one of my friends.

"We are with you," said the other, nodding in agreement. I looked at them, smiled and started walking faster. As I was crossing the other group, I looked for the right moment to lean a little to my left. My calculation was right. My shoulder brushed slightly against their leader as his jump was coming to a completion. He swirled, looked at me in anger, then looked back to see whom I was with.

Upon judging that they were more in number, he shouted, "Hey you, BC, can't you see where you're walking?" I stopped, turned, and my right fist connected fast with his left jaw. The next moment, he was on the ground – blood trickling from his mouth. His friends started for me, but my friends had reached there by then.

"Let it be an even fight — one versus one, unless you want to have broken bones as well," my friends said. The four others looked at them and understood that they meant it. They looked at each other and slowly moved back. Now it was one to one. As the leader was on his hands, trying to get up, I found the right moment to kick him in his face and more blood spurted out of his nose. He understood by this time that fighting back would only get him more pain, and he slumped back on the road. I waited for a few moments to see if had had any more fight left in him, but there was none. He had thrown his towel. Satisfied, I started to walk away but turned around for a last word.

"Hero, don't use such abusive language when women are around. Be careful next time."

"Don't fret over things, you either change them or accept them."

Solve your problem or accept it:

a. Define/understand the problem
b. Find the root cause of the problem
c. List all possible solutions. Find the best. Think out of the box.

We waste a lot of time and energy on things we can't change, and accept the things where we can indeed bring about a change. To have the knowledge of our strengths and limitations makes it easier for us to decide the right way. Frustration sets in when we worry about injustices even without making the effort to lift a finger against them. If it is something we can change, we should, else we should simply accept it.

Our fight for change should be aligned with our goals or our principles.

"At times, it is wise to take a step back to jump the hurdle."

6.4 Bonus dilemma:

First half decade of this century was bad for the Indian tea industry. More than one third of the companies could not pay the workers' wages on time.

Durga Puja is a big festival time in the North East and is the bonus time for employees. Most companies arranged the finances to pay good bonuses, but not ours. Our chairman was well known for his tight fisted nature.

After a series of meetings, our chairman agreed to pay the minimum bonus, that too in installments. We were travelling back together after meeting with the local union leaders when he dropped the bombshell, "We will pay 8.33% in three instalments. Our finances are very tight, so this Puja we will pay only 2.33%." I knew the workers would tear me apart for it – a bonus in three installments was unheard of. We had a lot of discussion on this, but I always ended up either frustrated or exhausted by his stubborn patience. Nothing could inspire any emotion in him. He would repeat the same thing a hundred times, and with the same pace of speech that there was no money. The more logic or good sense I used, the more he enjoyed torturing me with his complete ignorance.

I was not getting anywhere in this matter and I had had enough. I thought of trying another way and said, "Sir, I was thinking of one thing." He looked at me with a mischievous patronizing smile. I continued,

"Let's pay no bonuses this time." For the first time, I saw a flicker of surprise on his face. "Since we have no money, let us ask the 1000+ workers to tell their spouses and children not to buy anything new this puja, or even celebrate it. Since it is my head which is most likely be split open by them, I am ready to take that chance. I just want my family out of harm's way, so please arrange for their air tickets."

"No, no, we have to pay as per the law," he insisted.

"But since we don't have any money to pay, let us not pay," I repeated.

"But we are paying them in three instalments," he said.

"In that case, where is that money coming from? Why are we taking any pains at all? For the sake of law? Let me try this one time and create history." This time around, he offered to pay in two installments instead of three. I still refused to bite and insisted on not paying any bonus, taking on the risk of inviting the wrath of workers, union leaders and government officials alike. Now the situation was the opposite; he was trying to convince me for giving out a bonus, while I had only one thing to say, 'No bonus this time.' We parted without an agreement. All other companies had announced their bonuses and I was waiting to see if my tactic had worked.

At last, and with almost no time to spare before the festival, I received a call from my chairman that he had been able to arrange the bonus money after great difficulty, and that we could pay in one go instead of installments. It had worked.

Improve your decision making

a. Find all the info, facts and timelines, then look at all possible alternatives

b. Mind the stakes involved; higher the stake, more shall be the involvement of the stakeholders

c. Be ready to accept the consequences of your decisions

For thousands of generations, we have lived with animals, and the other attacks you the moment you fear for your life. That's human nature; having no fear or showing no fear puts you in charge of the situation. That is when the others start fearing you and doubting their own superiority.

At times, even a small piece of information about the decision-maker can help us get the desired result. The fear of standing alone and getting undue attention from the government officials helped me get the desired result. Not paying that which is obligatory from a compliance point of view would not only show you in a bad light, but will also sever support from all stakeholders.

Taking an extreme standpoint may at times help getting the desired result.

"In a stalemate, creating a perception that you are winning can actually win you the game."

6.5 Government office and chai-paani:

Government offices have their own style of functioning, but one thing is common – the easy going attitude. It's in the air, in their looks, their movements, their tea and beedi breaks, even in the number of files on their desks.

I was in a Chandigarh college and my younger brother had to go for a hospital internship. My father told me to go and talk to the concerned person for my brother's internship at a hospital near our home. I was venturing alone into the world of grownups for the first time and knew that I would be judged by the result. When I spoke to a couple of friends about it, their advice was to offer them some *chai paani kharcha*.

I found the concerned guy in his office with a ton of files on his desk and, of course, no place for a guest to sit. He took his time to look up with a very dry expression on his face, but didn't say anything. I waited, as did he with the same expressionless eyes.

"Can you please inform me if this particular reference number has been given the internship posting as per his choice?" I asked.

"And you are?" came the response.

"His brother," I replied. "I can pay for your *chaai paani*," I blurted out and realized that it had not been very convincing. He raised his eyebrows but said nothing.

"Come next week," was all I heard.

"Next week on which day?" I asked.

"Wednesday."

I was there the next Wednesday and then Friday, then the next Tuesday, and another Tuesday, and more such days. I was fed up and angry, so I decided to go with a couple of friends this time. This time probably my high energy level and confidence made him look up faster than usual. He then looked at my friends who were dying to see some action. "Look mister, it is the last time that I am here, but consider two things now. First, we study here, so we can find the time to come here everyday. Second, we know your office timings, so we can be here every morning to welcome you with slaps downstairs and repeat the same treatment for goodbye. Also, these friends of mine can accompany your wife to the market and kids to school and back. They won't say anything, but just follow them at a distance. If you want to complain about this, please go ahead. You may also tell the SHO sa'ab that I send my greetings. Now, tell me by which date and time will I get what I want?"

"It is almost ready, only a signature from the boss and it can be sent out by post tomorrow."

"Great, please make sure that it is done by tomorrow."

And it was.

Negotiation Skills

a. Have the info about the person/product/service

b. Have the info about the customer's need/perceived need

c. Know your customer

Negotiation is not only about the quality and price of a product/service, it is knowing your customer first. It doesn't always have to be about what the customer outwardly wants either. We pay a policeman for things we don't want to happen, to avoid harassment and to maintain peace. We avoid legal fights as they are lengthy, and drain our finances and energy.

Work can be done by turning tables; offer the other person a way to avoid his own harassment.

"Management consists of the best utilization of all resources; especially the human resource."

6.6 Karan Singh and appointment letter:

In Tea industry during the eighties, if you skipped the club evenings (tea life was a bit lonely, so it was necessary to socialize), it called for trouble from the boss. One senior colleague did so and was called by the boss – Mr. Karan Singh. There was always some fear when entering the boss's large office.

"Sir, may I come in?" he asked hesitantly.

"Come."

"Sir ,you asked for me?"

"Yes, I did. Tell me, why didn't you come to the club yesterday?"

"Sir, I was looking after planting so it was important to stay here."

"Ah haan, okay. Go to your bungalow and get your appointment letter."

"Sir?" the colleague stuttered.

"Didn't you hear me? Come back with your appointment letter."

"Yes, sir," he said and hurried out of the office with a confused expression on his face.

After around fifteen minutes, he returned with his three-paged appointment letter. "Read it," came the order. He started reading it. "Aloud!" Mr. Singh shouted. When he was through with it, he was asked, "Has it been mentioned anywhere that we hired a 'chowkidar'(guard)?"

"No, sir."

"Then why do you have be one? Do you want to be one?"

"No, sir."

"Then don't become one. You have been hired as a manager (assistant) and your job is to manage efficiently. You have to be a leader who the workers trust, and you have to motivate them to work with full conviction, even in your absence. At any point of time, the workers are working at more than twenty places. Can you be present everywhere at the same time?"

"No, sir," came his meek reply.

"Good. Have you understood now the meaning of training others, reward and punishment, delegation of work?"

"Yes, sir."

"Good. What are you looking at me for like a bloody fool? Go back to your work now. We are not at the club, are we?"

Just being present and managing efficiently are two different things.

Management skills:

a. Planning/organization/delegation

b. KSA (Knowledge, Skills, Attitude)

c. Helping others develop

Everybody wants the best from his/her team, but without taking the pains to develop the team members. Everyone can do better, provided that he/she is given the environment to learn and grow. To delegate, we need to trust our colleagues, and for that we need to know not only their knowledge, skillset and competency, but also their self-esteem and attitude. We need to invest a little more today for a better outcome tomorrow.

Get better results by giving independence, responsibility and accountability.

"Success comes with a clear vision, unshakable passion, sheer perseverance and good networking."

6.7 Networking pays:

I was posted at Dhelakhat tea estate in the early first decade of this century. Early one morning at around 5 AM, I was informed by a 'chowkidar' that some people were stealing tea leaves from our garden.

A decade earlier, Assam government had incentivized small tea plantations and the locals planted tea in small land holdings from which they sold green tea leaves to be bought by leaf factories and tea estates. Stealing leaves and selling them was the short-cut to earn easy money by young boys.

I picked up my bike and reached the spot. Around twenty people with covered faces were plucking leaves from our garden. As while stealing, one plucked as fast as possible, which was a double loss for us. In addition to plucking the ready leaves, the thieves would pluck away even the small shoots which were not ready yet. The sound of my bike had alerted them and they were ready for me when I reached there. Most of them had a 'Daos' (an 12"-18" sword-like but wider instrument used for cutting bamboos and tree branches) in their hands. They started to encircle me and I had to make a choice – whether to go back or confront them. I chose the second option. If I had walked away that day, I never again would be able to stop the thieves, but I had to take the risk of being attacked without any follow up action for an outsider like me.

"Hello, listen all of you! I am giving you a chance to leave all the plucked leaves which you have stolen, and leave."

"What you will do otherwise?" one of them asked. They had called my bluff.

'He is right,' I thought. 'What the hell can I do with bare hands against twenty armed people?' They were drawing closer and I had to make a decision quickly. I decided to confront them for two reasons. First, they were thieves looking for easy money, and logically they wouldn't have liked to jeopardize their future by attacking me. There would have been repercussions if they attacked. Secondly, I had a good rapport with the locals, especially the 'gaon burras' (the village headmen – in Assam, there are no panchayats as every village nominates wise mature men as their representatives) who were respected and never antagonised.

They were coming closer to me gradually. 'So far, so good,' I thought. An attack would have been fast and swift, so perhaps they only wanted to talk. I thought hard of what to tell them without pushing my luck too far, but something which would be acceptable to them at the same time.

"We can't leave the plucked tea leaves, we have worked for it," one of them said. I knew for sure that they won't do that. The next best option was to convince them to not steal again. "And sa'ab, we are not thieves. We are just poor and have to take care of our families."

"Well in that case, I can help you. Come to the office tomorrow and I'll get you some work," I said.

"But how can we do that? You will come to know who we are in that case."

"Don't you worry. I give you my word that I will not give you away, especially when you want to earn by honest work. You know me, I am a man of my word."

We stood silent for some time. It was time to move on, as both had saved their face.

Networking

1. Communicate what is in a deal for the other person
2. Know the other person's interests and personality, and interact accordingly
3. Be in regular touch with them

For millions of years, we have lived knowing only a small group of people. Studies show that our limit to know people well enough to predict their reaction is around 150. Networking saves a lot of time, energy and money. When I need something from someone, I should either know him/her, or know someone who knows him/her. Approaching someone directly might often not get me what I want. The reason is trust. You rarely trust a stranger – it is matter of self-preservation.

Networking is the shortest route to get the desired results.

Chapter 7

Out Of Box Thinking

"Our limitations are an imagination of our minds."

7.1 Riddle of Knots and Throne:

Once, a king of a progressive kingdom died suddenly. He had no male heir who could succeed to his throne. The ministers and the chief of his military held a meeting to come out with a successor, but could not agree on anyone. One of the ministers came out with an idea of announcing a competition to find the right successor. Everybody in the council agreed on a proposal of tying a rope in front of the throne with many very difficult knots. It was then announced throughout the kingdom that on a particular date, participants could take part in this competition.

A lot of people from all corners of the kingdom came over to try their brain power and physical strength. Many could not open a single knot, some could open only one, and a very few could open two knots. Nobody could open all the knots. It was late afternoon and it seemed that the core council may have to find some other way to choose their king.

Then, an eighteen year old young boy walked in. He looked healthy of mind and body and confident in his stride. He stood in front of the throne, looked at the rope with the knots, then at the throne, took out his sword, cut the rope in one strike, walked to the throne and sat down on it. By one look, he had realized that it was not possible to wrestle with the knots and untie them all.

There was absolute silence in the court. People looked at each other and at the handsome young boy sitting on the throne. Council members nodded to each other and walked to the adjoining meeting room. Some were smiling, others were in a thoughtful mood. After a short discussion, it was decided that the boy sitting on the throne was the right person to lead them as their king.

And so, he was declared their king.

At times, we have to think out of the box to solve our problems.

Out of box thinking?

a. Things change – what has worked in the past may not work in the future
b. Gives us an edge in achieving goals
c. Helps us in innovation

From the beginning our minds are prepared to look at problems from a certain angle; within confines of trusted old methods. Only few individuals, families and institutions promote innovation and out of box thinking. We would have never reached where we are today if we would have been dependent on trusted and tried methods. English promoted clerical education as it suited their purpose; we produce more engineers as per requirement of our time – it suites certain people/organizations. They become part of the crowd; we remember only people who took unbeaten path and dared to defy the norms – from Alexnder to Gandhi.

We need certain kind of people to do certain kind of jobs; but a free mind looks for out of box solutions.

"To land on the moon, shoot for the stars"

7.2 Long term planning:

Every parent gets anxious for their kid(s) when the time for applying to colleges comes. The choice of colleges and courses, and whether he/she will get their preferred college/course becomes cumbersome, in addition to very different advices from friends, relatives, and neighbours.

I have always believed in long term planning, and knew that my daughter was not going to score 96% marks required to get admission into any of the good colleges in Delhi University, so I tried to convince her to take up shooting after high school. Earlier I had taken her for firing of weapons a few times and the instructors had suggested that she could be good at it.

She was not interested initially, but probably made up her mind after reading the cut-off percentages for DU after class 11th. There was no shooting range in Gurgaon at that time, but one opened shortly at Manav Rachna school which was very close to our house. She started practicing there three times a week and entered a competition within a couple of months. She won a bronze medal in the North Zone (7 states) and qualified for nationals too. This boosted her morale and made her consider this sport seriously for the first time.

She gave the trials for six colleges in DU and got admission through five: Stephen's, LSR, JMC, Hans-raj and Sri Venkateshwara, and got her choice of course as well. In the very first year, she won the team bronze at the All India Inter-Universities Shooting Championship. She was happy now, very happy.

Plan for long term, taking into account your strengths, competencies and choices available

Planning:

a. Where I am?

b. Where I want to be and when?

c. What resources I need to be there?

We are uncertain about our future; so we take short term decisions at the risk of losing long term gains. If we are asked to choose a gift of 10 rupees today or 100 rupees after one year, most of us would choose 10 today. But our future depends on our planning for tomorrow; we have to get education today to fetch a job tomorrow; upgrade our skills today for a better tomorrow and build relationships today for a secure tomorrow.

Always plan for future, but work hard today to be there tomorrow

"If you cannot convince someone, confuse him."

7.3 Yudhisteri sach:

Truth and lies are as old as the human race. We all speak lies to save our skin, and at times to save somebody else's skin. We also tell lies to gain more, to negotiate or just to spite someone. However, we feel guilty most of the times after speaking a lie. Some people with strong ethics and principals can't speak lies. 'Yudhisteri sach' is an alternate for them.

During Mahabharat, the Pandavas were facing a very tough time against Guru Dronacharya, who was very aggressive in foiling all moves by them. After all, he was their Guru who had taught them all they knew about fighting a war. They tried all possible means to defeat the Kauravas, but to no use.

The mood was gloomy that night in Lord Krishna's tent. "Well, we have to think of something to stop Guru, or we may never win this war," Arjun said. "All conventional methods have failed." He then looked at Krishna and said, "Bhagwan, you have solutions to all problems, please suggest something."

Lord Krishna smiled and said, "I have something in mind, but Yudhister may not agree to do it."

"And what is that?" Bheem asked. Yudhister did not look happy as he very well knew the naughty mind of Lord Krishna.

"As we all know, the biggest blow to any father is the loss of his young son," Krishana continued. "The only way to stop Guru Dronacharya is to convey to him the news of his son's death."

"But Ashvathama is very much alive," Yudhister said with a sigh of relief.

"Yes, I know," said Krishna, "But an elephant by the same name was killed today. What we can do tomorrow is that Yudhister will shout to Guru that Ashwathama is dead."

"But I'll never do that. You all know it, I never tell lies." Others volunteered, but Krishna said, "No, Guru knows very well that we are at war and are capable of such things. Guru will only believe it if it comes out of Yudhister's mouth."

"But I can't do it," Yudhister said.

"Okay, there is a way out," Krishna said. "You will say *Ashwathama mara gaya, nar ya hathi – pata nahin*." (Ashwathama is dead – person or elephant, we don't know.) Yudhister was still contemplating when Krishna said, "Look Yudhister, in the larger interest of humanity, you have to do it. It is not the absolute truth, but also not a lie."

He turned to the other brothers and said, "When Yudhister comes to the second part of the sentence, start beating the drums loudly so that Guruji cannot hear it. He would think that his son has been killed and will put down his weapons. That is the time when you all will have to push through with full force to do maximum damage to the Kaurav army."

And it happened the way Krishna had envisaged it.

How to influence others

a. Know your audience

b. Learn the art of storytelling/analogies

c. Be honest in approach

You can only influence others when you know your audience; not only understand their beliefs and value systems but also how far they would go to protect those. The better you know someone the chances are better to influence their decisions. It is not telling someone what to do but guiding the person in a subtle way to a place from where he/she can see what you him/her to see. Share your experiences, analogies and stories to take him/her to this place which can influence in a positive way to take the right decision.

The subject and person knowledge are a must to influence others.

"Anger costs both our health and relationships; but controlled anger gets us results most of the times"

7.4 Experiments with anger and patience:

I used to contemplate a lot during my university days and realized that I had started getting angry very often. A couple of times, I had fights with friends for no reason and knew that something had to be done. I promised myself that I wouldn't get angry no matter what happened. It didn't work. 'Now what?' I thought. 'Okay, so the anger may be a result of my ego. How should I kill my ego?"

I found a solution one day when a friend suggested that I work with him in direct sales. "Let me tell you, people will not open doors, will speak rudely or even just shut the door in your face," he told me.

"This is what I want," I decided.

And so, I started my first job–selling food processors (a combination of juicers, mixers, grinders and flour kneaders.) Door to door direct sales was considered the most difficult job, and did help me change my expectations about people and their behaviour. It was as I was told, with few exceptions when some aunties would offer a glass of water out of concern during those hot blazing days.

One heavily overcast evening, a handsome guy in his early forties opened the door, looked at me and then at the thundering sky, and invited me in for a drink. He was an Air Force pilot who had met with an accident and had left the armed forces early due to the injury. We exchanged stories, laughed and thoroughly enjoyed the evening. The job gave me an opportunity to interact with the real world, which I found not much different from my own small and protected one, as there were all kinds of people – greedy, nasty, selfish, but also kind, caring and guiding.

The other realization was my impatience, and to have a better handle on myself, I experimented again. When I came across in a newspaper for a tutor requirement for a 3rd grade student, I figured that I would have to be very patient for the role. It had to be a rich spoilt kid whom the parents couldn't handle, that is why they needed a tutor. I was interviewed by both the parents and was asked of my expectations on the fee at last. "I don't know," I said, "You decide." They were convinced to hire me, as it was not just a number for me and showed my seriousness for the profession. It was an experience in itself. The family grew very fond of me, and God! I must have gained a couple of kgs on my lean frame as I was treated with a small feast during tea time everyday. That job helped me develop patience as the kid would easily forget the simplest things and I would have to repeat it n number of times to her.

But human nature is complex, and I stopped going there suddenly. One day, when I was on my bike, a car overtook me and the passenger waved to stop me. The father of that kid stepped out and asked me with concern in his voice why I had stopped going to his place so suddenly. Even his daughter kept asking them about me. He said, "She is a shy kid, as you must have seen, and doesn't open up to everybody. She had become very comfortable with you. Please start again. If money is an issue, you name the price and I'll pay you." I told him that it was not about the money, but I couldn't tell him the real reason behind my experiment.

Most important things for students

a. Gain as much knowledge as possible – class rooms, books, extracurricular activities

b. Experiment – to find where your interest lies, who you are?

c. Form good habits – discipline, innovation, hard work

Education is influencing our minds to gain subject knowledge; these are our formative years. To make experts out of us, our education system emphasises more on discipline and we lose our out of box thinking; it teaches us what is already there. But this is also the stage when we go through the process of knowing ourselves; our passion; our skill sets and our goals. Our success in life would depend upon what path we choose and what habits we form as students.

Curiosity, open for experimentation and habits formed during growing years are our success quotients...

"Oral words may not be taken seriously, but written words always are."

7.5 Facing an Interview:

Sitting through a personal interview is an integral part of the HR profession, and having sat for thousands of interviews gives you some idea about the preparation of the interviewees. Still sometimes, you get a shock. Once we were interviewing for a mid-level finance profile and I smiled when I saw a page of OD (Organizational Development) experience on a candidate's CV.

My first question was, "Your CV says you have OD experience. Is it true?"

"Yes, sir," was his prompt answer.

"Okay, tell me the full form of OD." There was no answer.

"Okay, tell me in brief what it is all about. What do you do in OD?" His smile faded away and he just stared at me as if I was from some other planet.

"Do have any idea that OD is an HR function and not finance's? What made you put OD as an expertise on your CV?"

The answer was simple. "Sir, I requested one of my friends to help me with the CV writing. He put it here, not me."

How can one think of hiring someone who is lying on his CV? Could one trust a person who is providing something in written which is completely false? To cut the story short, having a job is a very important part of our lives and we have to be honest about our experience and achievements. Your CV should reflect that.

How to prepare for an interview:

a. Understand the job role and knowledge, skills and attitude required for it

b. To understand the business and culture of the organization; collect all information available

c. Prepare yourself by matching your Knowledge, Skills, Attitude and experience to their requirements

For any interview the most basic thing is to understand the match between your knowledge, skills and attitude and the organisation's requirement and culture. Being very successful in one organization may not guarantee the same result in another; the reason is organization culture, which may differ to an extreme point. The mismatch is expectations from both- individual and organization; and most of the time both are unsatisfied. Fairness on both sides helps for a longer association.

Understand the need of the organization and match your K, S, A to its requirement...

"Planning is always long term; for short term, there is *jugaad*."

7.6 Planning:

On 28th July 2016, Gurgaon – a millennium city and a corporate hub for more than 450 large companies – came to a standstill for more than twenty hours. Nothing moved on the roads, or even the national highway passing through it, except for a few cars lapping in knee deep water. People got stranded on the highway and spent the night without water or food. What went wrong?

One phrase–lack of planning. In other words, greed took over planning as the city was the milking cow. The amount of black money generated for approvals/NOCs from real estate projects was in thousands of crores per annum. The result was, approvals for all natural drainage outlets or low-lying areas for residential projects. Logically, one cannot think of flooded streets in Gurgaon, as it is an undulating landscape and not a completely flat area as the north of it. When natural water outlets were filled out for multi-story buildings, water had no place left to drain out into.

On December 1st 2015, floods wreaked havoc in Chennai. The reason was similar – lack of planning, or being blind to the reality for the sake of greed. Much of the city has grown without a plan, with no regard to water flows or anticipating extreme weather events. Then there was illegal construction of an estimated 1,50,000 structures in the city.

What might have been a tank, lake, canal or a river twenty years ago is today the site of multi-storey residential and industrial structures. More than 300 tanks, canals and lakes have disappeared in the last decade.

Most of construction has taken place over water bodies and on important drainage courses and catchments. For example, the Pallikaranai marshlands, which used to drain water from a 250-square-kilometre catchment, has been reduced to a 4.3 square kilometre from 50-square-kilometre not long ago.

Planning:

a. Where I am now?

b. Where I want to be and when?

c. What resources I need to be there?

Most of us lack long term planning; the reason may be a fear of not knowing what tomorrow holds for us. We believe in "one bird in hand is better than two in bush." Lack of planning is evident all around us; in our lives, cities and in political arena. We have to invest in today for a better tomorrow; and that investment is planning and its execution. From late seventies to late eighties a research was carried out by Oxford university and it was found that people who planned their career and wrote it down were doing 9 times better than who did not plan at all.

Planning for your life is the only path to achieve your goals...

"If you look deeper at the problem; solution is already there"

7.7 Attending and short lectures:

I was short of lectures in pre-Engineering and had a very tough time convincing my lecturers to let me sit for the final exam, as the condition for sitting in the final exams was attending at least 67% of lectures at Panjab University.

The next year, in the beginning of the session, I was sitting with a couple of friends and discussing this situation when one of them came up with an idea to solve this problem. "You know, the list put out at the notice board is of the students who have not attended two-third of the lectures. Suppose we do not go at all to a particular subject's class, then our names will not be written down in the attendance register. That means, our names will not be on the notice board either. And those whose names are not on the notice board can sit for the final exam."

"It makes sense, yaar," I said. "Let me try for one subject this year," and I tried.

I chose Maths as the subject for which I would not attend a single lecture. After pre-Engineering, I wanted to switch to Humanities, with Psychology as my main subject. When I shared this with my parents, they were not happy. Both of them were in teaching and decided that Maths was better for me as the demand for Maths lecturers was good in colleges. I tried my best to convince them otherwise, but couldn't make any headway. I asked them to let me have my own choice of subjects and promised to take care of my own expenses by working part-time, but this didn't work either. Ultimately, emotional blackmail from their end that they had done everything possible to support me made me agree to their demand. They had made it a matter of their prestige.

That year, my name was not there in the lecture short list, and so I sat for the exam without any problem. It was a different thing how much I had been able to prepare on my own.

Look for solutions in problems

a. Every problem has a solution
b. The solution depends on how we look at a problem
c. Look for innovative ways for a solution

We face problems on a daily basis. Some have easy solutions, while some look daunting. It depends on our knowledge of the subject, experience, timeline, resources available and networking skills to find the best solution. The approach depends on our belief, value system and attitude in addition to its urgency and importance. It is not unusual to look for the solution in a particular direction, thus depriving us of out of box thinking which may provide the ideal solution.

Our solution to a problem is easier to find if we look at it as a challenge...

Chapter 8

Fighting Against Odds

"Fighting for life is not a luxury; it is an inbuilt quality in our system."

8.1 Fight your way out:

It was 1988 when I was in a college in Chandigarh and one of my friends had a problem with the AISSF guys from Khalsa college. As was the custom at that time, both agreed for all in — meaning, to agree on a place and time to fight with all of their respective friends/supporters so that it could be sorted out once and for all.

Around thirty-five of us got together from different institutions and reached the agreed place using different vehicles: cars, bikes and autos. Around fifty of them were waiting on a ground near their hostel. Since it was their place, they had collected heaps of broken bricks, water pipes with attached taps, in addition to swords and hockey sticks. Most of us were carrying iron rods and hockey sticks as well.

The opponents were in a line around their far reaching weapons of broken bricks. We got together and then charged at a very high speed, dodging the bricks being thrown at us. One fell, then another, and the fight began — a fierce battle with sticks and rods, then hand to hand, blood dripping from many faces. It was all over within five minutes. The opponents ran back to the safety of their hostels, carrying back their injured. We carried ours. Two were admitted to a hospital – one with some serious head injuries. They admitted theirs — ten of them for cuts on heads and faces.

It happened so fast. We had only our reflexes to survive — rage to make the attack first, and the shouts to hide our own fear. There was no time for anything else, only to put fear into others' minds so that they either surrendered or ran away.

It is later, not even when you tell each other what heroic actions you took, but when you sit alone and play the whole scene in slow motion that you realize what really happened. You remember dodging a hockey-stick strike from your own and telling him that you are on the same team, damn it! One learning – all team members should have been introduced properly. We did not even know each other too well as we had all met for the first time that day.

The biggest learning — how had the scale tilted in our favour? What did we do that made them run away? They were more in number, more confident as it had been their home ground, they had bricks and stones to hit with and we didn't. They were as healthy and as young, had better weapons too, then what had been different?

And it struck me that it had nothing to do with the physical attributes, but was completely psychological. We knew we could not afford to lose the fight as we were in their territory. The moment we would have gone weak, it was certain that they would have dragged us to the hostel and the others would have joined in the fun of beating the shit out of us. It would have been horrible and fear would have taken control of our emotions. They would have enjoyed breaking our bones – one by one.

The reason it happened the way it did was because we couldn't afford to lose it. That brought the energy and fearlessness that turned into rage for striking fear into them. They were in their comfort zone, we were not; they had a way out, we did not. We had to put all in and could not afford to lose; that made us win.

If you really want to have something, burn all your bridges.

Affordability versus burning your bridges:

a. Can I afford to lose something?

b. What would it cost me if I lose a particular thing?

c. Is it something for which I can fight till end?

Survival is a natural instinct, and whenever there is a threat to our survival–we draw out every ounce of our reserve energy to overcome that threat. When we have burnt your bridges, there is only one way to survive; fight like hell. That conviction and bravery saves us from being decapitated and the cost of burning your bridges depends on what is at stake; if it is something you can afford to lose, then you don't burn your bridges as you may have to cross them over again.

Burning your bridges pays only if you are fighting for something you can't afford to lose...

"We are so blinded by appearances that we seldom recognize wisdom in common clothes"

8.2 Panchayati or lath:

I happened to call Deepu, a college friend who had shifted to Delhi and had started a business. It was 1991 and calls were made from STD booths. "How are you, Deepu?" I asked him and sensed a hesitation on the other end.

"Yaar, I am stuck in a problem. Come to Delhi as soon as possible," he said.

"What happened?" I asked.

"Long story. I had an issue with my partner. Just take the first bus tomorrow morning, I need you."

The next day, I was at his house in Pitampura by noon. Another friend Mandeep was there already. Deepu had limited friends as he was a complete introvert. The two of us were probably all he had. He was tense and it was rare, as he would never show his emotions. He told us the whole story that his CA friend had been cooking accounts and was caught. They had agreed to separate and had a meeting with the area trade association. Deepu had paid him half the amount of their Karol Bagh office, but he had come back to occupy the office with some gun totting wrestlers, as his father-in-law was a DCP (Deputy Commissioner of Police) in the Delhi Police.

"But how he can do that? What about your agreement at the association office?" I said. He looked down and said, "Actually, it was all verbal."

"But why so? Especially when your partner was stealing, how could you trust him on a verbal commitment? That was a mistake."

He agreed and continued, "But that is in the past now. Let us plan what to do now. Let us start from the present situation. The office is still occupied by the 'pahelwans', but my partner is in police lock-up due to pressure from the shop owners' association."

"Since nothing is in writing, it will be very difficult to prove your ownership in the court, which as it is a very lengthy process. It may take years," I said. "To get the office free of the professional goons is again equally difficult."

"I have asked my cousin to get some of our own goons. They should be here within a couple of hours," Deepu informed me.

"Well, let us wait for them in that case," Mandeep said.

Time passed slowly, and his cousin finally arrived with three people. Deepu and I could barely control our laughter at the sight of them. His thirty-five years old cousin had brought with him three old men. One was of an average height and in his mid-sixties. The other was also in his mid-sixties, but quite short and with very thick eyeglasses. The third must be approaching fifty, and was thin to the core. Mandeep looked at me and started laughing, "Yaar, I know we might be called cowards, but it shall be wiser to slip away now with an excuse, rather than face the DCP and the gun-wielding wrestlers, what do you say?"

"Na yaar, he is our friend so we have to stand by him. Let's see what comes out of it," I said.

Deepu shared all the details of the case with his cousin and his friends. Shortly, we were informed that we were going to visit the police station to speak to Deepu's ex-partner. It was getting dark by the time we reached the police station. Deepu's cousin seeked the SHO and we found him standing with a couple of people. The SHO introduced us to the DCP who was in civilian clothes. Now the focus was on the DCP and arguments started. Temperature started rising. Deepu and I were silent spectators, while Deepu's cousin handled the situation and we admired him for it. He was rather good at convincing.

"DCP sa'ab, there are only two ways to settle a dispute; *'panchayati or lath'*–one is the social/legal way, while the second is by the force of power. Now you tell me, how do you want to settle it? My cousin has already tried the first one through the association, but we can still try it. It is not too late." When he got no response, he carried on, "We have just come to Delhi and this is your area, but let me tell you one thing DCP. You are a senior person in the Delhi Police, but there are many others who are senior to you as well. We all know how difficult it is to get an audience with the PM. Different CMs have to camp for days in Delhi to meet him. I am a nobody, but I can meet him tomorrow morning if I want. Do you know how? The contractor for his housekeeping service is my uncle." He continued, "Forget about anything else, give me time till tomorrow noon only, and after that if you so much as even touch my cousin's office with your little finger, that office is yours."

There was silence as everybody was trying to weigh the others. The SHO intervened and invited all of us to his office, "What will you have, tea or cold drinks?"

After sometime, it was decided to have a meeting the next morning at the Association's office. Deepu's cousin got up to shake hands with the SHO, after which we left.

The next morning, we were just starting for the meeting when I saw all three of the older people carrying guns, two revolvers and a sawed off double barrel. I whistled, at least we were ready to face the other party.

We reached on time and waited for quite some time for the others to join, but there was no sign of them. By the end of an hour, Deepu's cousin had again impressed everyone by his analogies, stories and incidents.

At around noon, we decided to carry on as the DCP and his party was nowhere to be seen. I was among the last to get down from the first floor of the association office and stopped as I saw around a dozen wrestlers with broken ears walking towards us from the other side. Deepu's cousin told them that they were late for the meeting.

"Meeting for what?" their leader asked.

"To settle the dispute."

"Disputes are not settled this way," the pahalwan replied and took out his pistol. "The dispute will be settled the way I want it to be settled." Mandeep was asked to inform the other members of our team, as they were ahead of us and had reached the corner by then.

I held my breath and looked around for a way out. There was none. I was scared to die so young. Most of the pahalwans were armed, while I could see only one revolver with the senior citizen of our team. The other two had walked ahead. The odds were against us.

The senior *tau* on our side held the pahalwan leader's gaze and said, "Son, you are young and your whole life is ahead of you. Your kids must be very young, they will need their father. I have lived my life and wouldn't mind falling to a bullet. Even a whole life in jail will still keep you away from your family and kids. If you really are ready to kill for a completely wrong reason, here, take my gun."

There was complete silence; just edginess, darting eyes, and slow breathing. Either side was preparing itself mentally to run or pull out the guns. The pahalwan leader thought for a moment and relaxed – a good sign. He had been presented an accurate account of the possibilities, and saw no threat from our end.

"Where are you from?" the tau asked.

"Jaunti," came the reply.

"Do you happen to know fauji?"

"He is my guru."

"He is like my younger brother. Ask him when you see him the next time."

By this time, the other tau with the thick eyeglasses arrived. He looked around and asked me where the DCP was.

"What happened tau?" I asked him.

"I want to slap him tight. Who promoted him to be the DCP? He is more of a goon.»

More silence followed. The pahalwan leader wrote down his contact number and passed it on to tau. He said, "I will speak to you in the evening, please call me." Then, he turned and walked out with his team. That was all. We heaved a big sigh of relief.

It is not always numbers or weapons which turn a situation in our favour. It is rather the wise decisions and the best use of our strength. In this case, it was the experience, and communicating that you have nothing to lose.

Truth versus Perception

a. Truth is what we believe in

b. Perception is our own interpretation of things

c. Except universal truths, perception becomes our individual truth

Truth is universal, perception is individual; our perception at times can only see a part of elephant instead of whole picture. And perception makes us believe what we see and what we want to believe in; just a look and we decide about a person as he/she seems to us and not as that person is or could be. A sculptor does not just see a stone but what it hides within it – a beautiful sculpture.

We only believe what we want to believe in and not what it is...

"Just breaking rules doesn't get you anywhere; you have to make your own rules:

8.3 Passport office Gurgaon

There was a cultural exchange program at my daughter's school and she was one of the students selected to visit a school in Germany for four weeks. But there was a problem – her passport had expired. My wife had been after me for some time for her passport renewal, but I kept postponing it, thinking there was no immediate plan for a foreign trip. Not much time was left now. I was in a fix, but was confident to sort it out as usual.

We applied for a renewal online. My wife and daughter visited the office the first time, stood in a queue for more than three hours, and were asked to visit again. The second time, I didn't want to take any chances, so I approached the SDM, who was known to one of my friends, for verification and a letter of introduction. He was very helpful, but warned me that they still might ask for his ID card's copy, which he didn't have at that time due to his recent transfer to Gurgaon.

Again after around three hours at the office when our turn finally came, the guy looked at my documents and called his senior. The lady indicated that my document could be fake, which let me off my handle. "Ma'am, since you have accused me of forgery, please file a complaint with the police. Can you tell me who hired you in the first place as it is clear that you don't really know anything. This is the second day that we have wasted here, and for what? I have my passport, my wife has one too. Since children's passports expire in five years instead of ten, why would you punish us?" My voice kept rising with each sentence and soon I was shouting at the top of my voice — which can make people tremble. "I know you will keep stalling me for no reason till I go outside and pay your touts six thousand, but let me tell you, I am not going to do any of that. It is not because I can't pay, but because I won't pay as a matter of principle. I don't know about you, madam, but my forefathers have fought for this country as freedom fighters. You can issue passports to Bangladesh migrants on their arrival, but not to people who have been here for thousands of years and have fought for it? I want to see your passport officer, and now!" I was so angry that everybody stopped working, and quite a few applicants came to my support as everybody was going through the same cycle of frustration and anger.

In the same form, I walked into the passport officer's room and was soon thumping his table. "The police can't handle me sa'ab, please call the army in case you don't issue this passport today." He asked me to sit and ordered cold drinks to cool me down. He looked at my wife and said, "Madam, you should keep your husband a little more cool." He pulled out an office manual and showed me a clause, requesting me for one more verification.

"But your online appointment system is awful," I told him.

"Sa'ab, please don't worry. Give me time and I'll see you as per your convenience."

"Fine," I said. "But I work in a private organization and cannot take leave every second day."

"You won't have to. Madam and your daughter can come."

The new passport came within five days, as promised by him.

Anger versus controlled anger:

a. Anger makes you blind, but controlled anger can get you results

b. Make sure you are 100% right before you use theatrics

c. Be reasonable to give the other person a way out

Anger is a negative emotion; it blurs our vision and we start hitting at shadows. It consumes our energy without getting us any results. But at times, we have to show anger to get a desired result; we do it with kids and at workplace to elicit a certain kind of behaviour. And when we do so, we have to be very careful that it is limited to a certain degree, as there is always a chance to go spiraling away in case the other person also responds with anger.

Always leave a way out when you use controlled anger to get things done.

"Being in the right gives you unfathomable courage"

8.4 Courage or stupidity:

A boy just after his 12th, shifted to Chandigarh from Bihar and was staying with a friend of ours at the University hostel. One day, five students walked into their room with hockey sticks and iron rods. They started beating Mahender. The boy got scared and ran to their balcony on the 2nd floor. A couple of them followed him. The boy got so scared that he held the balcony railings to jump, but couldn't. It was high and there was a concrete floor below. One of the attackers hit him on his knuckles with the hockey. He let go of the railing and fell two floors below. He had a backbone injury and had to be admitted into a hospital. The injury was serious.

Mahender did not know any of the group members who had attacked them, neither had he any idea of who might have sent them. We had a lot of discussion on this, suspecting that a girl could have something to do with it. "Did you become friends with somebody recently?" I asked him.

"No," he said.

"There can't be any smoke without fire. Think again."

After a couple of weeks, Mahender came to us and said, "I have found out who sent those guys."

"And the reason?"

"Well, it is too early to share, but I have been talking to a girl, my classmate. She is a pandit, and as you know, I am from a lower caste," Mahender said.

"But hitting on the knuckles of a teenage boy who was already hanging from the 2nd-floor balcony was inhuman," I said. "Let's teach that bastard a lesson."

The guy who had sent the group to attack was also on a 2nd-floor room, but in a different block. One day at around 2 PM, we were informed that he was in his room. Five of us went to his room and knocked. He must have been expecting a reprisal, and didn't open his room. The room adjoining his was open, so we entered that room and went to the balcony. The guy was standing there, fear written clearly on his face. I asked him to open the room, but he just kept standing there. The balconies at Panjab university hostels are in an arc shape and there is at least a 3 feet gap in between. I knew, if we went back that day, we might not get another chance. There was a good possibility of that guy taking to his heels for a couple of months, or even worse, a compromise by involving somebody who we may not have been able to say no.

"There is only one way in. I'll cross the balcony and open his door," I suggested.

"But look at the gap, Kundu. It's too dangerous, and if the other guy pushes you, we could be visiting you at the hospital too," a friend whispered in my ear.

"He looks too scared, so the chances of him pushing me are very thin. I need just a few seconds. Be at this corner and if he tries to do something, just hit him on his head. I just need a window of a few seconds," I said and handed over my hockey stick to a friend. I got up on the balcony railing and put my hands on the curved wall to cross it. It was a huge bloody gap, very difficult to cross even without the fear of another person's light push, but those were our carefree days and we were naïve. I tried to put my other foot on the other balcony. Just a little more stretch and I could make it. My eyes shifted from the balcony railing to the walls and then to the guy standing frozen. I decided to jump back to the first balcony at his slightest movement. My leg was on the adjoining balcony's railing, my hands still on the curved brick wall. The next second, I crossed over to the other side with a jump. I had a huge sigh of relief, then walked into his room and opened the door.

Everybody rushed in with abuses and strikes of hockey sticks and rods. He covered his head with both his hands and sat down in a foetal position. In less than two minutes, he cried aloud. It was a cry of fear mixed with pain, and we stopped hitting. Blood was spurting from his head — somebody had hit him on his head in that melee. Hitting the neck and above was not in our code and it made me furious. I asked who had done it, but none replied.

The guy ran out of his room and then downstairs with his hand over the head wound. Blood was dripping all over the stairs. One good thing about Panjab university is that it sits just in front of PGI – one of the best medical institutes in North India. His wound was sure to be taken care of. It was time for us to disperse and go invisible for some time.

We knew the chances of an FIR being filed by the other guy were very high, and had to arrange for minimum damage. One of my school juniors had his uncle in the police at mid-senior level. When the investigation officer came looking for us, he had his instructions. I had to go for my SSB for armed forces, and when I came back to the university after ten days, I knew that things had not been sorted out till then.

I went to the police station and asked the IO politely about the matter. "I have been to the hostel a couple of times, but never found the guy," he told me. "Let's try one more time," I said. He agreed and we came to the hostel in a police jeep. The guy was in his room luckily. He was picked up and we went to the police station again. The guy was scared shit.

"There is nothing to worry about," I told him. "You did something inhuman and got a taste of your own medicine. What you need to do now is just take your complaint back. Let us finish this NOW!" He was relieved and did as was told.

"It is not just how strong you are; it is your strength versus your adversary's"

a. Take stock of your strength
b. Take stock of your opponent's weaknesses
c. Strike at weaknesses of your opponent

Strength comes from various sources; belief, knowledge, skill sets and being right. When you believe in someone or something, you fight for a cause; a cause you believe and it puts you on a stronger wicket. It is your passion to fight for justice which makes you brave as you are fighting for a bigger cause. It makes you fearless and you are ready to take chances otherwise you may not have.

Be strong and be fearless when you decide to fight for a cause...

"Management is knowing competencies of your team members and nuisance value of your foes"

8.5 The Boss:

My first job in Tea was in Tripura where I had the chance to work with an exceptional boss, soft-spoken but firm, blessed with a sharp memory, emotional genius, impeccable integrity and ethics, risk taker and a master of behavioral understanding. He knew exactly how one of his team members would react in a particular situation and assigned jobs accordingly. He would also come to know how one of us was feeling and never delayed in connecting to change one's feelings from negative to positive. I learned from one of the best managers.

One afternoon, I saw a couple of vehicles and a few bikes parked in front of our office and a group of people standing there. It meant trouble, and I was sure of it as my boss had decided to cut down on 'Durga Puja' donations drastically. Durga Puja is a holy festival in Bengal and Tripura, and every year more than 50 clubs from a small nearby town would descend for donations. Boss decided to pay just two of them and that too after making them realize that it was not their birth right. "You see, it puts us in a better bargaining position," he said. We were very skeptical and the reason was that there was only one bridge connecting us to the town. In a tea estate, we might be safe, but not in town, and almost every day we needed something to cross over. Violence was common in that area due to proximity of international border with Bangla Desh. In last assembly elections one person was hacked to death in broad daylight and with hundreds of spectators watching.

When I reached the office, the tempers were already high. Boss was surrounded by around 14-15 people who were threatening him. A couple of them had small firearms in their hands. Boss, like always, was completely cool with a hint of smile on his lips and was trying to calm them down. "Look, son, I am just a person who is managing things here; as you know, the company is in loss, but I already have informed my superiors in Calcutta that they need to send funds immediately. I will try my best to push harder and sent you the donations the day I get it," he said.

"We know you don't want to give us donations, otherwise how have others before you been giving it to us for so many years? Don't take us for fools, else we will send you back to where you came from," their leader said. He was tall and looked every inch a rouge character; it was clear he meant business. It went on for another 20 minutes, but the boss kept on repeating the same thing without any change in his tone — polite with a hardly discerning smile. The others gave him a timeline and left. Suddenly, it was all quiet, very quiet.

When I had joined that estate in the early nineties, I became aware early on about the practical problems of being very close to the international border with Bangladesh. People on this side would kill somebody and cross over. Bikes would disappear and were smuggled by tying underneath large bamboo bundles floated in rivers, and hundreds of those would cross over every day. People from the other side stole cows and any other valuable thing they came across. Also, rebels would get trained in Bangladesh and would cross over with automatic weapons.

Once, I saw a crowd of angry people on my way and stopped. Four young men were being brutally beaten. On asking, someone was told that those were Manipuri rebels and were trying to sneak away in the wee hours, but had been caught. When asked why there were not handed over to the police, they said, "You take care of your own business, sa'ab. Don't try to intervene, it could be bad for you as well. We know the police will release them after taking all their money and weapons to be resold in the black market." For the first time in my life, I stood there while those people were being hacked to death. I could not watch after the first one took a blow on the head and crumbled to the ground, dead. Those villagers were no longer human. They had taken a different form, an animal form of hyenas, thirsty for blood.

When I had joined, I was a bachelor, so could take some risks. My boss had a very good relationship with the Deputy CM, and many times the SP would send an official to inform him that there was rebel movement in our area and he should not stay at the estate for the night. Somebody had to stay back, and I volunteered every time. I would keep my sports shoes on with loose knots, and a torch and a sword by my bedside. I had told all the watchmen to use a particular whistle sound for thieves and another one for rebels. "You should never try to confront them, just pass on the message for the kind of danger," I had repeatedly told them. I was clear on what to do in which situation. For thieves, I would come out charging with the sword, and in case of rebels, I'd put on the shoes, take the torch, dash away to labor lines and hide there till the danger was over.

My boss gave me a choice after my marriage. "Look, Ramesh, you were alone earlier. I could ask you to stay back, but now you are married and carry responsibility on the home front. It is your choice now, although I would insist you to stay in town whenever a rebel movement is there." It is a different thing that we stayed only once in town, didn't like it, and continued staying at the estate instead. After I changed my employers and shifted to Assam, one of my ex-colleague got kidnapped from the same bungalow where I had been staying earlier, and was taken across the border. A few months after that, my ex-boss was picked up at night while his wife kept pleading that he was aged and sick.

He remained captive for around one and a half months, but asked the management to not pay for his release.

"Your strength lies in your conviction for a cause"

a. Knowing what you can get away with is a bliss
b. Knowing the boundary of your opponent is an added advantage
c. Being confident in adversity wins you the battle

Being thousands of kilometres away from home, near a porous international border demands more compliance to local culture. Your ability to assimilate and your networking skills will determine what stands can be taken. It also depends on support from your team members and other stakeholders; if they also believe in a cause you believe in, it becomes easier to get what you want.

Know the limits of your adversary to decide how may steps to take to challenge him/her.

"It is your reputation which determines who you are."

8.6 The morning police:

For around five years, I was posted in a tea estate which was very near to the Dibru Saikhowa forest area — home to the ULFA for a very long time. As this jungle was neither motorable nor could be accessed by boats, it was ideal for the ULFA training camps. The area was not considered safe. In addition to the ULFA, it was also prone to the attacks of dacoities. There had been a couple of such incidents when I was there, and they targeted the bungalow close to the river bank each time as it was easier for the dacoits to get away from there in a boat without any worries of getting followed or chased.

Initially, I was in a bungalow just adjoining the factory. It was considered the safest as manufacturing would start at mid-night and 100 plus workers would be working the whole night. After a couple of years, I was promoted and shifted to the river bank bungalow.

One such afternoon in the early winter season, I was at my bungalow when received a call from the factory bungalow that some armed dacoits had been at their gate and had gone towards the factory. "Okay, don't worry. I'll just make a call to the police station and will be at factory in five minutes." I started for the phone to call the police station. The officer at the other end heard me out before connecting me to his officer in charge. The OC advised me to go out and have a look at the dacoits to find out their number and the kind of weapons they were carrying.

"And how much time will you take to be here?" I asked him.

"Sa'ab, you know we are short of staff and cannot move out without CRPF support. CRPF is short of vehicles most times. Also, it will be dark soon and we cannot take the risk of venturing out into the dark. We can come under attack from the ULFA, or could be hit by mines. We will surely be there first thing in the morning tomorrow."

"What about my people?" I almost shouted, but then controlled myself as my shouting would not have helped solve the problem, their presence would have. "In that case, I want to speak to your SP."

"Okay, but you will receive the same response," was all I heard from the other end.

'Let me go out and tackle the problem myself. I can't depend on these jokers,' I thought and started out.

When I reached the factory bungalow, the lady there was quite shaken, as the dacoits had fired a couple of rounds at the factory gate, but no harm was done as they didn't enter the bungalow. From there, I started for the factory. I had no fear as I knew if they had wanted to harm me, they would have come to me directly.

By the time I reached the factory, the dacoits had gone and there was no one at the gate. I had to shout a couple of times before the *chowkidar* (guard) came and opened the gate. "What happened?" was my first question.

"Sir, they are at least a dozen and are carrying firearms. They asked me to open the gate. When I didn't open but asked what they wanted, they simply fired in the air. I got scared and just ran away. They simply shouted that they will come again and went in that direction." He pointed towards the river. I spoke to a few other workers to make sense of it all or find out who they were and what they wanted, but got nothing valuable.

I went to my desk to call the SP, but got almost the same response that it was getting dark and he wouldn't put his peoples' lives at risk. "I'll arrange a police team to be at your place by six in the morning, and I'll ask the OC to file a complaint over the telephone so that you don't have to come to the police station. You can sign the FIR in the morning on their visit, and get a copy of it as well," he said. I thanked him for his help and put down the receiver. Now, I had to arrange for additional guards for the night and wait for the morning.

In the morning, the IO came with a team and started writing down the FIR. It was all right, but he paused and put down his pen when I told him that two shots had been fired. "How do you know that those were gunshots and not firecrackers?" he asked.

"Because I can very well distinguish between these two," I replied.

"No, it must be firecrackers," he insisted.

"Okay, let me tell you, I am fond of shooting and have fired more than a dozen kind of weapons, from a 9mm pistol to an LMG. Those were rifle shots, and you can ask others witnesses around if you want. That is what I told you guys yesterday that two shots were fired," I said.

"But I can't write that in the FIR. You see, as per the police manual, we have to respond immediately in case of shots being fired anywhere. My job would be at stake. Sorry, but I can't write that." He had a stern look on his face. It went on for a few minutes and finally a compromise was reached to use the words: *I heard a shot-like sound.*

The first question that came from my bosses was how come the safest places were attacked and not my bungalow, and whether I had orchestrated it?

It was most likely my reputation which made me safer. I had made sure everybody knew that we never kept any valuables or cash at our bungalow. Also, I had created myths about my short temper and fearlessness. Of course, this was in addition to my fairness in dealing with all matters and respect for all individuals.

Internal Versus external factors:

a. You have control over internal factors but not external ones

b. Try to come up with internal solutions if there is no external support

c. Accept the challenge of external non support

A leader stands for his/her people during the time of challenges to provide them strength they need to face such challenges. Confidence building and making right decisions without fear will increase your acceptability as a leader. One can only choose from choices available and in absence of outside support you have to be strong enough to find next best solution internally.

Testing time for leaders are when limited resources are available...

"Fighting against all odds makes you strong. It is the challenges that bring out the best in you."

8.7 The Brooklyn Bridge

The Brooklyn Bridge, connecting Manhattan and Brooklyn, is 1825 meters long, has a span of 486 meters, is 85 feet wide, and is at an average height of 277 feet above water. It was the world's first steel suspension bridge and an engineering marvel of its time. It stands as a tribute to the triumph of one man's indomitable spirit and his determination to not be defeated by his circumstances.

Prior to its completion, the only way to travel between Brooklyn and Manhattan was by ferry. Its chief engineer John Roebling started working on plans to build a bridge over New York's East River to shorten the travelling distance in as early as 1857. It took him almost fifteen years to sell this idea which was considered almost an impossible feat at that time. In 1867, the state legislature chartered a company to build the bridge, and the work started in 1869.

While conducting surveys for the project, John Roebling sustained an injury that resulted in a tetanus infection. The tetanus took Roebling's life just before the construction began, and his son Washington Roebling took over as his successor at the age of just 32. Not long after taking charge of the bridge, Washington Roebling suffered a paralyzing injury as well–the result of decompression sickness. He was left with a paralyzed body and brain damage which made him bed ridden and speech challenged. He could not move, walk or talk.

The situation looked hopeless, but Washington Roebling still had a burning desire to complete the bridge. He tried to inspire and pass on his enthusiasm to some of his friends, but they were too daunted by the task. His wife Emily Warren Roebling rose to the occasion and provided the critical written link between her husband and the engineers on-site for the next eleven years till the completion of the bridge. Under her husband's guidance, Emily had studied higher mathematics, calculations of catenary curves, strengths of materials, bridge specifications, and the intricacies of cable construction. The work continued in spite of such huge challenges and the bridge was completed in 1883. This was a victory of human spirit against all odds.

Fight all odds till you complete your task.

Face your problems:

a. Face your problems as they appear; procrastination doesn't help

b. Find reasons for your behaviour – is the task difficult/time consuming/boring

c. Find a simple solution; truth is always simple – only lies have webs

We don't look at things as they are; we either pre judge or ignore them at our own peril. Most of the times procrastination is the reason for ignoring or delaying; the reason could be anything from absence of deadline, availability of inadequate resources, not knowing where to begin with, overwhelming task; or fear of failure. It is always better to tackle the problem as it appears rather than waiting it to grow in a herculean and daunting challenge.

Tackle each problem as it appears; postponing only makes it more complex...

"Be ready to take risks for the outcome you need"

8.8 The Beer Story:

During one of the summer vacations, I was visiting some friends in Rohtak, and the six of us were sitting and making small talk. It was a June afternoon and was very hot. In the late eighties, ACs were not very common. The next best way to make hot days bearable was to have a couple of beers. We totalled our pocket money, but it was insufficient to buy those many beers without missing payment of our hostel mess bills. Somebody suggested going to Tilyar lake as a solution. There was a bar and a restaurant at the lake run by the government and they had a store at the back. We could manage to take away a crate of beer from there. There was a discussion on the number of people being around, possibility of police personnel being there during day time, how to make it happen, how to carry along the crate, and so on.

"We'll need three bikes. Since we already have two, will borrow the third one…" and so a plan was made. "We'll have to park them near the store, but with a free passage. We'll develop a plan after an assessment of the place."

We reached there at around 4 PM, but it was still very hot. There were a few people under the trees by the side of the store, as most visitors were away near the lake for boating. We found a place to park our bikes from where we could get away easily. There was a door at the rear of the store through which consumables were being carried in and out. The task looked easy except for one problem, there were two policemen sitting on the lawn under the shade of a tree.

After taking a round, we came back to our parked bikes. Tarzan (a dare devil friend with the built of Tarzan) said, "I will go inside to pick up the beer crate; Kundu comes with me in case somebody tries to stop me. Rajeev and Ajju will be with the bikes running, and Deepak and Dhruv stand behind the policemen in case they try to stop us. Kundu!" He turned to me and continued, "In case someone tries to stop me, just punch him hard to knock him out. Dhruv and Deepak, you should not let the policemen get up. Just threaten them so that they don't stand up. In case they try, just push them hard on the ground and run for the bikes." He looked at us and asked, "ready?" We all nodded. Our blood had started pumping hard and we were ready for action.

I followed Tarzan into the store and there were stacks of beer crates there. Tarzan saw a revolving door that led into the kitchen. He kicked it hard as someone was coming from kitchen knocking down the person on the other side, for we heard a crash. He picked up a crate and dashed for the door leading into the front lawn. I was ready like a boxer to take care of any obstacles, but we were our before anybody else could know what had happened. The policemen heard shouts from the kitchen and tried to get up, but Dhruv and Deepak standing right behind them warned them not to move. Within a minute, we were on our bikes and shot out of that area.

"Hurray!" we shouted as we shortly reached the highway, clear of all danger. A slab of ice was bought on the way to chill our beers in a bucket.

Those were the tastiest beers I have ever had.

Taking risks is:

a. Planning

b. Putting yourself in the line of fire

c. Keeping an escape route

Getting away is more important than entering the 'charkavyuh' which is a planned strategy and so you have to plan as well for an escape route. You have to look at all possibilities; every small detail matters. You have to be deeply observant for any changes required as per emerging situation; your mind has to take in all around you and ready to make changes in real time.

Plan for a goal but be ready to bring in changes on the way, if required...

Chapter 9

Being Right Versus Peace of Mind

"It is better to buy peace with your spouse and your boss than being right."

9.1 50th Anniversary of an American couple:

An American couple was celebrating their 50th wedding anniversary and had invited over a few close friends. One of the husband's friends asked him, "Tim, would you mind sharing the secret of such a long union with your wife?"

"Oh, that's very simple," Tim replied. "On the very first day of our marriage, we agreed on a simple principle – all small family matters will be decided by Linda, whereas my word would be final on all important matters."

"Wow, that's great," the friend said. "But how do you decide which matters are small and which ones important?"

"Easy again," said Tim. "Small matters include which house to buy, which colour to choose for the house, the kind of furniture we want, which car to buy, name of our kids, which school they should go to, which club membership which should have and other such small things."

"Okay, what are the important things then?" the friend asked.

"All matters of great importance like whether the US government's decision to attack Iraq was right or not, whether the President was right in bailing out banks like J. P. Morgan Chase and Goldman Sachs, and whether all this technology is good or bad for us."

Being right and buying peace

a. Nothing is permanent – look at the larger picture

b. Let go of small things today for a larger goal

c. Peace comes with understanding, not confrontation

Peace comes with understanding the larger picture, and it certainly is not for free. We have to pay a price in terms of realigning our expectations with our goals in life, letting go of the past and forgiving ourselves/others for deeds done, trading one thing to have another, giving back to the society, accepting others as equal and being just. We shouldn't just look at what we don't have, but also what we have and others don't. We need peace of mind to build our families, institutions and societies.

Look inside to find peace, outside lie all temptations.

"The solution to a problem depends on how you look at a problem in the first place."

9.2 Salesperson's dilemma – no market or huge market:

Around fifty years back, an American shoe manufacturing company sent its Sales Manager to one of the African countries to expand its market share.

They received a telegram: "No market as nobody wears shoes."

During the same period, another company had sent its Sales Manager to the same area. The Sales guy went around the country before confirming what he saw and sent a telegram: "Huge market, nobody wears shoes here as of now."

Glass half empty or half full?

Cost of opportunity depends upon:

a. The way we look at things, do we see problems or opportunities?

b. Do we look at things as they are, or the things that can be?

c. What is our first reaction: grab an opportunity or run from the problem?

All of us have a different perception of the world around us, and give meaning to it as we perceive it. Success depends on whether we see problems or take them as challenges to turn them into opportunities. If we take things at their face value, we may miss the hidden opportunities and the positive outcomes that can be. We have to grab every opportunity we come across to make a better tomorrow.

Don't just look at things as they are, look for what they can be.

"Only numbers and size may not take you there, patience and intelligence will."

9.3 Spanish Armada

Queen Elizabeth ascended the throne of England after a long civil war. Her dream was to bring economic stability to England and was slowly building its foundation. The King of Spain, Philip II, was a devout Catholic and considered it his personal mission to bring England back to Catholicism from Protestantism. He was building a large armada to invade England.

Elizabeth was against raising a large army as it would be a huge expense and would disturb the growing economy of England. To delay this inevitable war, she decided not to provoke Philip but to damage Spain's economy. She sent her greatest naval captain, Sir Francis Drake, in secret to act as an independent pirate and invade the Spanish ships carrying gold. This delayed Philip from repaying the loan that he had taken from Italian bankers for his shipping and war expenses. This also delayed the ship building armada for around six years.

At last in 1588, the Spanish armada was ready and sailed to England with 128 ships, 2000 canons and 30,000 sailors and soldiers. By this time, Elizabeth was ready and had raised an army to confront the Spanish attack. She knew the Spanish army was still way superior in fire power and numbers. It seemed difficult to win either at sea or on ground.

There was a lot of discussion on war strategies to neutralise the looming threat. Somebody came up with an out of the box idea.

As the Spanish ships were anchored in a very close formation, it was decided to fill England's eight ships with inflammable material, put them on fire and ram them into the Spanish ships. As the ships gathered full speed and were about to crash, the sailors evacuated their ships. It created havoc and resulted in complete chaos, causing dozens of Spanish ships to catch fire. In trying to save their ships, many more collided with each other and were damaged badly. The loss was huge and the morale of the Spanish plummeted. The invasion was called off. Only one third of the ships and men returned to Spain. The rest lay at the bottom of the sea.

Preparing for win:

a. Find the underbelly of a problem

b. Build up you strength

c. Have patience to strike at the right time

There are many ways to win a war. More than physical strength or numbers, wars are fought on a psychological front. Wars need large finances, hate for the enemy, material gains, technological support/ latest weapons, etc. One can weaken the enemy by an indirect attack on their financial institutions, spreading contradictory rumours, bringing down the morale of the fighting forces and uniting your own people in preparation of your defence. It brings larger participation and support for your decisions.

If you can't win in direct confrontation, weaken the enemy financially and psychologically.

"A true leader will connect to you instantly."

9.4 Tea stall and a helicopter ride:

In one of the by-elections for the state assembly, I had the chance to come in contact with Choudhary Devi Lal in the early nineties. It was just after he had been Dy PM and was canvassing for the Kalka by-elections. 'Tau', as he was fondly addressed, was staying at his favourite guest house in Morni hills. His tall and healthy frame was putting a lot of strain on his knees in his old age. Every evening, he would be served hot water for massaging his feet, after which he would go for a walk.

One such afternoon, there was an election rally happening very close by, and Bhajan Lal was addressing the gathering. We could hear him while sitting with 'tau'. He laughed off Bhajan Lal, and simply said, "He is lying."

After the evening tea, he asked us to accompany him for a walk. After around 400 metres from the guest house, we came across a roadside tea stall. It was just a shack with a couple of rough wooden planks placed on bricks, serving as benches. "Boys, it has been long since I have had tea here. Let's have a cup of tea," he said and sat down on one of the benches. "Dharma, how are you? How is your family? All well? Make some tea for all of us," tau said.

Dharma retorted that he didn't want to speak to tau. "What happened to you? Why don't you want to speak to me? What have I done?" tau asked.

"I don't want to speak to you because you took the sarpanch along with you in your car sometime back, but didn't offer me a ride. Do you know how happy I would have been if I was seen by people sitting with you?"

Tau laughed, "Oh! So what? Don't worry. I'll take you along for a helicopter ride this time when we form the government," tau said.

"Oh no, tau. I don't want to go for a helicopter ride."

"What happened now? Aren't helicopter rides are much better than car rides?"

"Yes, but who will notice me sitting in a helicopter? I want to be seen sitting with you," he said and we all laughed. His intention was nothing else but to be seen with tau. It speaks a lot about a leader's integrity and sense of pride his followers feel by their close proximity to their leaders.

Being a leader:

a. Know your followers
b. Treat them with respect
c. Keep feedback channels open always

A leader knows his followers and the followers trust him/her. It's a two-way engagement. The basic qualities of a leader include being a visionary, having the communication skills to share that vision with their followers, being grounded to know what people really want, having respect for his followers/audience and accepting feedback without being judgemental. The problem comes when you distance yourself from the majority and build up walls with a small door through which only a few can enter. Slowly, you grow distant from your own followers, and the decisions you make are based on information which is not authentic. Everything starts falling apart then.

As a leader, keep yourself available to your followers and earn their support for your vision.

"If you can speak the language of your audience, you already have won the battle."

9.5 A gateway to the heart:

I was around 10 years old when, on a hot June day, I found lot of excitement in the people around me; almost everybody in the village very excited. On enquiring, I was told that 'tau' was coming to address people for the upcoming assembly elections. Everybody was heading towards one place – the rally ground. I also started to hear 'tau' — leader of the masses.

It was all dust and chaos at the venue. Thousands of people had come to hear him out. People were standing on rooftops, walls, bullock carts, and tree branches to get a better view. Kids sat on their fathers'/grandfathers' shoulders. Shortly after, there erupted a wave of excitement as people started shouting, "Tau is coming, tau is coming," and then the slogans, *"Jab tak suraj chaand rahega, tau tera naam rahega."* (as long as sun and moon shine in the sky, you will be remembered)

Shortly, tau reached the make-shift stage to address the gathering. After an initial address, he came to the main subject and his vow of waiving off the farmer loans. He said, "I have seen people being dragged off in jeeps as they are not able to pay their loans back. Where would they earn the money to pay back the loans when rains have been insufficient and crops have failed for two consecutive years. Have you ever seen an industrialist being pulled away from his children? What kind of justice is this? A poor farmer is jailed for a few hundred rupees, while crores of rupees are lost in the non-payment of loans by rich industrialist, but there is no prison for them." His words received a roar of approval.

"The opposition asks me how I would waive off the farmer loans. My answer is simple – when I am the Chief Minister, I'll get all the farm loan files, write '*karze maaf*' (loans waived off) at the top and sign Devi Lal at the bottom." The crowd went mad with joy, clapping and cheering, "Tau Devi Lal zindabaad!"

This is what the public wanted to hear, for their problems to be sorted out by just a signature of their leader.

Grounded leaders:

a. Know the pain of their followers

b. Offer practical solutions

c. Give them confidence and belief

The best machines in the world are the simplest ones. Simple solutions to complex problems are accepted easily and by all. In fact, most complex problems have simple solutions–if only we have the strength to go for them. To keep the masses entangled in complexities works for leaders for their own gain. Democracy involves taking along the majority with you, so your appeal must be taken in a positive way by the majority.

As a leader, you win the trust of your followers by promising them simple solutions to their complex problems.

"What we want to have and what we should have are two different things."

9.6 Wishes versus reality:

In one of my previous organizations, our Chairman asked us to hire an Executive Assistant. The JD read, 'hiring not a person, but many persons put together in one; a person with great leadership skills, project management skills, financial skills, communication skills and vast industry knowledge.' The other problem was salary, as it was only one fourth of an EA available in the market.

After a long search, he liked somebody and hired him at a salary five times the initial budget. The person left in five months. Reason–the Chairman would call him at one in the morning to arrange for a vehicle to drop his guests (radio taxi service hadn't started yet), all his suggestions would see the dustbin, his habit of asking a lot of questions, etc.

Here, the problem was not the hire, but the huge difference in the actual tasks that the person had to perform, versus the idealistic personality that the Chairman had in mind. In other words, there was a complete mismatch of competencies. The solution was simple. He wanted a smart secretary, not an Executive Assistant. We could have avoided the waste of time, energy and finances, had we gone for a competency mapping exercise for the said role.

Competency Mapping is the process of identification of competencies required to perform a job successfully. It is done by breaking a job role into activities (including the smallest activities), grouping similar activities and skillsets required to perform these activities efficiently.

A similar problem is faced while trying to find a match for one's son or daughter in an arranged marriage. We never try to find what qualities will make their union successful, but look for an ideal person: an educated and earning *bahu,* but who is also rooted in the family values, or a simple *bahu* who also earns a good salary; a successful damaad who returns home before it's dark, or a simple damaad who earns a lot.

We look at idealistic people, but not people with the right competencies and compatibility…and we pay the price for it.

Be able to differentiate between needs and wants:

a. What do I need?

b. Why do I need it?

c. When do I need it?

Many relationships break due to unreasonable expectations when we use two different yardsticks for ourselves and others. The purpose of any relationship is always mutual, there has to be understanding from both ends. At times, what I need is completely different from what I desire, but I want the best, not what will work for a long time – and there lies the problem. I want to give the minimum but want the best, always forgetting that the other person also wants the same.

Needs and desires are two different things.

"Accept that some pain is inevitable for peace of mind."

9.7 150 slaps and swollen faces:

I was in a boarding school in eighth class. The house captains and prefects were from 9th class. They would often look for reasons to make an example out of juniors in the name of discipline. One such diktat was to speak in English at the hostel.

One fine afternoon after lunch, all 7th and 8th class hostellers of our house were asked to be present in the change room. We were asked to stand in a semi-circle and were told that it was a subordination not to speak in English.

"BCs, you will do as you are told. You did not carry out our orders to speak in English. Now, the first boy from the left will slap each person five times and will take his place at the right end, and this will continue till each of you has had your turn," said our house captain.

Everybody's faces looked ashen. I calculated the number of people in that semi-circle. 'Thirty into five is one-fifty. Fuck – we are screwed.'

The start was tepid as we hesitated slapping our friends with full force, but the seniors were ready to call the person out and slap so hard that everybody understood the consequences. And so it went on, and 150 slaps later, our cheeks were burning and swollen.

The world is not always just. We have to accept the injustice if we are not strong enough to stand against it.

The definition of pain:

a. The threshold of physical pain depends on our mindset

b. What doesn't kill you, makes you stronger

c. You endure it to look strong

Pain threshold is different for different people, and it depends upon either on our beliefs or the cause we are fighting for. To accept pain is a sacrifice for a better tomorrow, or a desired result today. A poem immortalised by Ram Prasad Bismil is a fine example of sacrifice for a better tomorrow, "*Sar faroshi ki tamanna ab hamare dil mein hai, dekhna hai jor kitna bajuay kaatil mein hai.*" (the desire to make a sacrifice is in our hearts; let us see what strength lies is in the arms of our executioners)

Don't fear the pain. Draw a bigger line of your beliefs/value system/goals by the side of the line for pain, and it shall automatically become shorter and bearable.

Pain is inevitable. Accept it for a larger cause, and it shall become bearable.

Chapter 10

Limiting Beliefs

"Our decisions make us what we are."

10.1 Decision Making: An Art

Decision making in organizations is very complex. Most of the times, we arrive at timelines without taking in account the speed required, and at times the direction changes, and we are not even aware of it. If clarity on both these elements is there, then the need of resources to take it to a conclusive end also becomes clear.

There are many practical nuances in real life. Many times, we make decisions first, and then look for justifications to prove those right. Else, we find someone else to put blame on.

At times, we go with no risk policy and take no decisions at all. Worse, we procrastinate and take bad decisions at the last moment for lack of time.

We often spend a lot of time on very small decisions and are left with no time for important ones. Even worse, at times we take decisions which someone else at a higher level would like and put the organization in a precarious situation. We don't want to be seen in negative light, so we support the decisions which we know won't bring the results we are looking at. The list goes on, we take credit for decisions we didn't take, and disown the decisions which didn't go right.

Basic questions to be asked for right decision making:

- Is there clarity on purpose of the decision?
- Is it in line with the vision of the organization?
- What is at stake? Large stakes need larger involvement of stakeholders.
- Are we looking for long term or short term gains?
- Can we validate the facts gathered to take a decision? Use check-sheets.
- Have we looked at all alternatives? Have brainstorming or SWOT analysis exercises been carried out? Have we consulted all who would be affected by the decisions we make?
- Have we looked at the pros and cons, timelines and financial impact?
- Are we ready to accept the consequences in case it doesn't bring the desired results?
- Have responsibilities been clearly defined and communicated for its execution?
- Do we have a process to monitor the progress and feedback mechanism in place?
- Do we reward people who take initiative in decision making, or do we have a culture of finger pointing in case decision does not bring expected results?

The best way to get a decision accepted is to initially put the idea in the mind of stakeholders and then support it when it comes back to you. This way, we get maximum support from all involved.

Use logic and reasoning rather than basing decisions on emotions; right brain versus left brain? Most of the times, we take decisions based on emotions rather than logic, our likes or dislikes, to put somebody down, too soon or too late, or choose not to take any decision at all.

What prompts a person to take decisions would differ for different personalities. Being a leader means to encourage decision making. To get the desired results, four things to be looked into are: clarity, responsibility, timelines and risk involved. To get the best out of team members/colleagues, it is important to know their personality types, or in other words, what motivates them.

Of course, it is not the same in all organizations or with all individuals. Legacy carries an important effect on decision making. The sentence that *this is how it has been carried out for decades* is very common. The culture of an organization, the average age group of employees, gender mix, education level etc. will make a difference to a large extent. It is human nature to grow cautious with time, but also within the same age group, the risk-taking capacity would vary to a large extent.

To sum up, what should be done to encourage decision making a rewarding process? And the most important things would include: to clearly communicate the importance and timelines, to share information on data collected, to involve all stakeholders, to provide adequate resources, to create a mechanism for monitoring the progress and feedback, reward and recognition for decisions bringing expected results, brainstorming in case of different results, celebrating successes. In one sentence, create a culture where decision making is encouraged.

Decision making truths:

a. Culture plays a big role in decision making
b. Fear of wrong decisions makes us indecisive
c. Timelines and stakes are important to take into consideration

"Our success depends on our self-awareness, how we manage ourselves in present and how we develop ourselves for future."

10.2 Self: awareness/management/development:

Emotions drive our behaviour: we smile when we feel happy, we cry when we are sad or fearful, we make sacrifices for people we love, we shout because someone made us angry. Without a doubt, our emotions dictate how we feel, think, and behave.

Self-awareness is knowing what emotions or feelings drive our behaviours. Each of us lives in our own version of "reality" — our interpretation of things happening around us. Emotions are natural, but our ability to control our reactions to situations is something we all possess, but few are able to effectively manage.

According to Daniel Goleman, the competencies associated with self-awareness are:

- Emotional self-awareness: recognizing your emotions and the impact they have on your life.
- Accurate self-assessment: identifying your strengths and limitations.
- Self-confidence: knowing your worth and capabilities.

Self-awareness can be of two categories.

The first is internal self-awareness–how clearly we see our own beliefs, values, passions and their impact on others.

The second category - external self-awareness means understanding how other people view us in terms of these same factors, taking others' perspectives to understand where we stand.

Even though most people believe they are self-aware, only around 10% of people actually fit the criteria. Research has found that experience and power can make us overconfident about our level of self-knowledge.

Self-Management

Self-management is the ability to understand and regulate our own emotions, and use them to guide our behaviour towards positive outcomes. This means, although we cannot dictate our feelings, but sure can dictate our behaviour. Nothing makes us angry, we get angry; nothing makes us hopeless, we decide to feel hopeless. We are the masters of our own minds, so we should dictate how our emotions make us feel, not the other way around.

Emotional intelligence affects the way we manage our behaviour, navigate social complexities, and make personal decisions that achieve positive results. Emotional intelligence is made up of four core skills that pair up under two primary competencies: personal competence and social competence.

Personal competence is made up of our self-awareness and self-management skills. It is our ability to stay aware of our emotions and manage our behaviour.

Social competence is made up of social awareness and relationship management. It refers to getting along with others well, being able to form and maintain close relationships, and responding in adaptive ways in social settings.

Roosevelt said, «Men are not prisoners of fate, but only prisoners of their own minds. They have within themselves the power to become free at any moment." This means, we are free to stop reacting to events and emotions and learn to choose our response to any situation.

Self-Development:

What was relevant yesterday is no more so today, and what is relevant today will not be so tomorrow. We need to develop ourselves for tomorrow to be relevant. The first important thing for self-development is a vision, where you want to be, when, why and how?

We have to take responsibility to start self-development. That means, exiting the comfort zone, reviewing our habits and developing new positive habits. Remember, excellence — not perfection — will help take us there.

Our ability to effectively survive, thrive, and lead comes from flexibly riding out our ups and downs. Learn from the past, plan for future, but focus on the present – be in the moment.

Comfort in uncertainty–nobody can say with certainty what is going to happen tomorrow in this complex and ever changing world. One needs to be comfortable with uncertainty.

Most important things for the self:

a. Self-awareness
b. Self-management
c. Self-development

"Our limiting beliefs are our biggest enemy on the path to success."

10.3 Limiting Beliefs

Beliefs are essentially assumptions we make about ourselves, about others and about how we expect things to be in our world. We have all these theories, ideas, and explanations about how things are and how they ought to be, all of this helps us make better sense of the world around us. We all crave a sense of certainty as it provides us with peace-of-mind and helps reduce stress, anxiety, and fear. It's a fundamental human need that builds the foundation of all our belief systems.

Beliefs are not facts; however, deeply ingrained beliefs can indeed be mistaken as facts. These beliefs are often conclusions we have drawn based on our childhood experiences. Back then these beliefs may have served us–the reason for holding onto them for so long. For grown-ups, these beliefs may become a hindrance as they are no longer compatible with our life or our goals. Our life has changed but our beliefs have remained constant, which is why we feel stuck in the present.

Beliefs are formed throughout our lives, we collect facts, evidence, and references that help us form our idea of reality. Over time, we build up more references through the use of our imagination, through the knowledge we acquire by personal experiences, and through the influence of our peer groups. These references help us form ideas about things, which turn into opinions, our opinions eventually turn into beliefs. These beliefs are still flexible in the early stages, however, over time as we keep collecting more references these grow stronger.

Eventually, we reach a certain stage in the evolution of each belief where it becomes so deeply ingrained and rooted in our nervous system that our expectations can no longer be changed. This could be in spite of overwhelming contradictory evidence that proves otherwise. And this is where a belief turns into a conviction.

When there are no available references to lay down the foundations for a belief, some people turn to faith. Faith is merely a belief about something that has insufficient real-world references supporting it. We have faith because we desperately want to believe something. And when we desperately want to believe something we will ignore the facts and instead use our imagination to help create the references we need to support that belief.

Convictions are the strongest beliefs and are often immune to logic. They are beliefs that have the highest unwavering certainty, commitment, and dedication. Convictions are beliefs that we have built over a lifetime and support by a tremendous amount of references.

Beliefs that got us to where we are today won't get us to where we want to be tomorrow. Our beliefs must, therefore, change with the times, they must also change alongside our goals. If they don't change, then we don't change, and our goals will always remain out of reach.

How to overcome limiting beliefs:

Identify your goals: Your first step is to find out what it is you want. What are goals, objectives and the outcomes you would like to achieve?

Identify your limiting beliefs: If a belief serves you and supports the goal you are working toward, keep it. However, if it doesn't serve you and hinders your progress, then this is a clear indication that you are dealing with a limiting belief.

Understanding the Formation of Your Limiting Beliefs: Understanding how these beliefs came into existence can help you work through them more effectively. Most likely these beliefs are linked to childhood memories and experience. Unlocking these memories can help you to find the root cause for letting go of specific experiences.

Letting Go of Your Limiting Beliefs: All limiting beliefs are formed with good intentions to protect you from pain. They might protect you from short-term pain, which unfortunately often leads to long-term pain.

Preparing for change: Reduce the intensity of limiting beliefs by gathering facts which state otherwise.

It's important to note that some of your limiting beliefs may, in fact, have some basis in reality. These beliefs are not based on assumptions but instead upon facts. If they are based on facts, then you will need to treat these beliefs as "problems" that must be solved. They are in essence the physical obstacles that you must overcome to clear the path to your goals.

3 things to come out of limiting beliefs:

a. To know our goals
b. To know our limiting beliefs
c. To form new beliefs in line with our goals

"Fear stops us from utilizing our full potential"

10.4 Overcome your fear

If we are absolutely fearless, we wouldn't survive for long. Ignoring oncoming trains, jumping off rooftops and playing with poisonous snakes will certainly kill us. In the course of human evolution, the people who feared the right things survived to pass on their genes. In passing on their genes, the trait of fear and the response to it have been beneficial to the survival of our race.

Fear is of two types: physical and psychological, physical fear is an inbuilt mechanism in all species for survival but psychological fear is imaginary and taught to us for better performance.

The brain is a profoundly complex organ. More than 100 billion nerve cells comprise an intricate network of communications that is the starting point of everything we sense, think and do. Some of these communications lead to conscious thought and action, while others produce autonomic responses; fear response is autonomic.

There are two paths involved in the fear response: The low road is quick response, while the high road takes more time and delivers a more precise interpretation of events. Both processes happen simultaneously.

Anticipating a fearful stimulus can provoke the same response as actually experiencing it. This also is an evolutionary benefit; those humans who felt rain, anticipated lightning and remained in the cave until the storm passed had a better chance of not getting struck with thousands of volts of electricity. Experiencing fear for our safety is normal. But living with chronic fear can be both physically and emotionally debilitating.

Fear extinction involves creating a conditioned response that counters the fear response. It starts with small steps and continues until new, fear-extinction memories are formed.

How to control fear:

1. Learn about the thing you fear. Developing an understanding of what you're afraid of goes a long way toward erasing that fear.
2. Train yourself, start small and work in steps, slowly building familiarity with a subject of fear makes it more manageable.
3. Talk about it. Sharing your fear out loud can make it seem much less daunting.

"Only discipline in depression will get you out of negative thoughts"

10.5 Control your negative thoughts:

Our thoughts are formed by how we perceive things, depending on our experiences and our interpretation of those experiences. For example when you were young and someone told you or gave you the impression that you weren't "good enough" at something; until that moment you might not have thought that about yourself, but now that someone else's thought has made its way into your mind, and as it was not challenged, so you accepted it as true. After some time you start taking that belief as your own. That negative thought will remain in your subconscious mind and you might be not beware of it, until something or someone triggers it.

There are two parts of our mind, working together: the conscious and the subconscious, the conscious part of our mind is responsible for logic and reasoning, and a good portion of our negative thoughts, the subconscious part of our mind is responsible for all of our involuntary actions. Our breathing and heartbeat are controlled by our subconscious

When a negative thought comes to our mind, it usually triggers an emotion, like sadness or anger; the conscious mind monitors whatever thoughts arise, and serves as a filter to either accept or reject them. What it chooses to accept or reject has a lot to do with what thoughts seem useful or beneficial for one's sense of 'self' or 'identity'. So if you have a negative opinion of yourself, you will allow for negative thoughts to come in and stay there, which your subconscious absorbs as your beliefs, and those beliefs will stay real for as long as you allow for them to.

Most of our beliefs are formed in our childhood, when we are susceptible to be influenced by adults around us and do not realize when our thoughts become our core beliefs. In that age we wanted to be liked and accepted, so go along opinions we may not agree with and over a period of time it becomes our thought process. Lot of negative beliefs we carry about us may have been initiated by someone else and can be false. But we are not aware of it. It is conditioning like tying a rope to young elephants, they try to break it and when not able to, grow up with a belief of rope being stronger than them, whereas it is not. This belief makes them not to try at all after they have fully grown up and can easily break it.

Question and challenge your negative thoughts, ask who said it? You? Or somebody else? Negative opinions and beliefs could be a result of not being successful in overcoming a challenge in the past. But we change, what did not work earlier may work now as we have gained knowledge, skills, experience and are in a better position today to overcome those challenges.

Overcoming negative thoughts:

- The first step is to accept the existence of a negative thought, denial doesn't help.
- Be aware of a negative thought rather than reacting to it

- Find its roots, revisit your beliefs and value systems, who initiated that thought in the first place, was it you or somebody else?
- We should challenge our negative thoughts now as our Knowledge, Skills, Attitude and experience have changed
- Take time to turn it around to positive
- Keep yourself away from negative environment/ people

Control your negative thoughts

a. Accept that negative thoughts are natural
b. Find what triggers these thoughts
c. Go to beliefs and value systems and work out a plan

"With money we buy things we like, and that makes us happy"

10.6 Can money buy happiness?

I remember buying a soft plastic ball with pictures on it for my 2 year old daughter. And I still remember she was so happy with it that she played with it continuously for around an hour. My whole family was happy and excited when I bought my first car. I remember so many times being happy when I bought so many more such things.

I am certain money can bring happiness, but the only kind which takes care of uncertainties about our survival and basic comfort. The problem is, most of the times we mix up happiness and peace of mind; happiness is temporary and peace of mind is a state of being. Peace of mind achieves happiness but it is not true not vice versa.

We can find happiness in small matters but peace of mind takes more than that, peace of mind comes from looking at the larger picture and a control over wants and desires.

We have been told otherwise, but why everyone who tells us that money cannot buy happiness wants more of it. What they are telling us is that money cannot peace of mind, but it can definitely buy security, comfort and happiness.

Happiness depends on:

a. Health

b. Wealth

c. Relationships

"If we do not bring balance in our lives, chaos takes over"

10.7 Balanced life:

There are people who go all in for their beliefs and then there are majority like us who create a balance without taking extreme risks. There is nothing wrong and right but just different attitudes and different circumstances. Here, let us talk about the second kind.

10 things where we need to strike a balance between:

Demand and Supply: From finances to health: strike a balance between demand and supply for long term favourable results

Change and Stability: Static and Dynamic qualities: keep core values unchanged while changing strategies

Emotions and Logic: Make decisions based on logic but without losing human values

Work, Family and Self: Divide time between three looking at a long term perspective, to lose 1 at the cost of other 2 doesn't pay

Innovation and Discipline: We just survive by disciplined working without innovative thinking

Winning and Accepting: To keep peace at times it is better to accept defeat from boss/spouse than winning

Push and Pull: Pull works better most of the times but not always, push but after creating a pull

Democracy and Autocracy: Democracy doesn't work always, at times we have to put our foot down

Leading and Following: Start working on leadership skills while being a follower and understand your followers while being a leader

Short and Long Term: At times we have to let go of short term gains for long term achievements

Balanced life: strike a balance between

a. Emotions and reason: when to decide emotionally and when to use reason
b. Static and dynamic: keep basic principles intact while changing with time
c. Self, family and work

"Find happiness in small matters and happiness finds you in all matters"

10.8 Is happiness my goal?

We, humans started settling around 12,000 years back with the advent of agriculture. Prior to that we were nomads and foragers staying in small groups and had to compete with animals. Our primitive ancestors must have felt weak and vulnerable in fighting/competing with animals for food. Some animals were very large in size, some others had speed, and some other sharp teeth and claws. To overcome this imbalance they formed groups to defend themselves against predators and for better hunting; it also provided them psychological protection. Large groups offered humans safety and freed some for inventions for better efficiency. The fear of being weak and alone was overcome by staying together in villages and cities.

The upward journey of mankind began with invention of machines. The axe, wheel and pulley were the initial simple machines which made our ancestors lives easier. The scientific revolution from mid eighteenth century has changed our lives drastically. Cure for various deadly diseases, steam engine, telephone, electric light, printing press, microscope, radio, airplane, satellite, computers, internet, cell phone, censors, Robotics, AI.

Till beginning of 21st century machines have made our lives easier, convenient and helped us achieving unthinkable otherwise. But now we have started wondering whether they will control our lives in near future? Or will machines replace us in the long run? Drones as delivery boys, driverless cars, robots, machine learning/AI are already a reality, what next? The experts say that within next ten years 30 – 60% of jobs in various sectors will be taken over by machines and the degree will vary from industry to industry. Machines are likely to replace humans where repetitive work is involved. Robots are already doing jobs like cutting, welding and assembly operations with lesser mistakes and better quality. This also saves cost in the longer run. But experts believe that some jobs in every sector where human touch is required will have more value and cannot be replaced at least in near future.

But my concern is a bit different. It is not that what percentage of jobs will be taken over by machines, as we always have found alternate ways to engage and earn. Also as we have seen in the past when we were freed from one level of jobs we had time to create jobs of higher level, from agriculture based to manufacturing, from manufacturing to services, better R&D and knowledge based solutions. In future also we will come up with higher knowledge based services.

Also my concern is not will machines become dangerous but my concern is that we humans will become machine like. Our basic definition of social beings is already changing as businesses have no room for emotions and emotions have been our identity. Already we see people don't find time to talk to their family members or friends. This initially creates a lot of stress as it takes few generations to adapt to completely new way of life. Also we are distancing ourselves from nature, we are boxing ourselves in our own small world with virtual reality.

All work and no play/fun will take us near machines, meaning we will slowly become like machines.

At the pace things are changing we may be last generation where majority are humans as per original definition; with every generation percentage of machine like human beings will increase exponentially where emotions will not only value less but will be frowned upon. And this is happening more in large cities where not only we are part of a blind race but also don't have time for family/friends. Probably we may have to fear machine like humans more than machines themselves.

The science and technology has made our lives comfortable but has again separated us from families and social groups. Today our closest companion is a machine – mobile phone; this has made us venerable again and this time it may not be predators but stress... Stress is taking more lives today than hunger. What tomorrow holds for us is imaginable...

And the solution lies within ourselves, we may have to go back 5000 years and as then find time to start reflecting on our actions. We have to start looking inside our minds and not just outside for finding peace. Also we have to revive our connect with nature. Let's reflect and be close to nature for happiness, being machines like may bring efficiency but will also bring huge stress.

3 biggest challenges for future:

1. Not to become machine like in thoughts and activities
2. To be able to pick relevant information out of unverified and unauthenticated trash
3. To be able to bear stress

10.9 Happiness:

Is my goal in life to be happy? And what would give me happiness?

1. Time spent with family/kids/friends?
2. Achievement at work?
3. Appreciation in social/work circles?
4. Pursuing hobbies/social work?
5. Amassing money/power/assets/toys?

And what do I do for all this?

We work and live in cities where stress is a part of life, and small towns lack opportunities. The best case scenario would be earning as much as we are in cities and staying in calm place but as that is not possible. Second best option is to create a balance between these two. To make decisions keeping larger picture in mind, plan for future and take action on our plans, share and care, give some space to others and develop self to develop others.

Let us try to decode happiness:

H	**Hear**	Out what others to have say before you speak (we learn by listening, not by speaking); Learning makes us happy
A	**Act**	On plans made & written down (we learn by doing); Succeeding makes us happy
P	**Plan**	For your tomorrow (we are the result of our decisions); Planning today would make us happy tomorrow
P	**Patience**	Is the mantra (Taj Mahal was not built in a day); Calmness makes us happy
I	**Invest**	In relationships (returns are only on investments); Fruits of investment makes us happy
N	**Nurture**	Others (we learn best when we teach); Sweet fruits of our planted trees makes us happy
E	**Evolve**	Times are changing & so should we (change is the only permanent thing in our lives); Change makes us future ready & that makes us happy
S	**Share**	With less fortunate (see how happy are children after sharing); Sharing makes us happy
S	**Self**	Self awareness/self management/self development is the key (develop self to develop others); Being better today than yesterday makes us happy

"The biggest problem with us is that we try to find peace outside; it only lies within us"

10.10 Achieving peace of mind:

Peace of mind depends on our ability to calm our thoughts, having a handle over our emotions, let go of things we can't control, not worrying about what others think about us, having reasonable expectations, our ability to forgive, to let go of past, develop patience and tolerance, being close to nature, having meaningful relationships, contributing back to society. It is a result of our beliefs and value systems (our desires and wants), our self and social awareness...

It depends on our reaction to things happening in our minds or around us. Each person has his or her own thought patterns. They are the result of experiences we've been exposed in the past. We use these thoughts to label events either positive or negative. We want some things and if we don't get them, we are unhappy; and if we get what we wanted, we then fear losing it – it is unending process.

Our thoughts keep us from living in the present moment, which is another way to describe having peace of mind. But rather than to push them away, the key is to learn how to handle our thoughts when they come up. After all, they'll most likely keep coming up until the day we die.

Don't hold grudges. Learn to forget and forgive. Nurturing ill feelings and grievances hurts you and causes lack of sleep.

Don't be jealous of other people. Jealousy and low self- esteem often leads to lack of peace of mind.

Accept what cannot be changed. This saves a lot of time, energy and worries. We must learn to put up with such things and accept them cheerfully.

Don't dwell on the past. Let bygones be gone; forget the past and focus on the present moment.

Learn to be more patient and tolerant with family, friends and everyone else.

Don't take everything too personally; a certain degree of emotional and mental detachment is very helpful.

Learn to focus your mind. When you focus your mind, you easily forget worries and anxieties, refuse to think negative thoughts.

Meditation helps

How to achieve peace of mind?

a. Understand the difference between happiness and fulfillment

b. Have a plan for life based on your beliefs and value systems

c. Give back something to society, your time/ knowledge/finances